NAUTICAL RULES OF THE ROAD

Editorial Assistance by Cheryl Matherly Bothwell
Illustrations by J. M. Schu

NAUTICAL RULES OF THE ROAD

The International and Inland Rules

THIRD EDITION

B. A. Farnsworth

Larry C. Young

CORNELL MARITIME PRESS

Centreville, Maryland

Library of Congress Cataloging-in-Publication Data

Farnsworth, B. A., 1949-
    Nautical rules of the road   :   the international and inland
rules   /   B. A. Farnsworth, Larry C. Young. — 3rd ed.
      p.   cm.
    ISBN 0-87033-408-5   :
    1. Inland navigation—Law and legislation.   2. Rule of the
road at sea.   I. Young, Larry, C., 1952-   . II. Title.
    KF4188.F37   1990
    341.7′5666—dc20   89-71243
                                            CIP

Manufactured in the United States of America

First edition, 1981. Third edition, 1990

CONTENTS

ACKNOWLEDGMENTS

In the preparation of the first edition of this book we received assistance from a number of quarters, but we are particularly grateful to the following individuals for the professional expertise, comments, and constructive criticism they so willingly rendered to make this book into a useful tool for the mariner.

Captain J. E. Ferguson, U. S. C. G., Commanding Officer, U. S. Coast Guard Institute; Commander E. J. Geissler, Master Mariner, Maine Maritime Academy; Lieutenant Commander J. L. Hassall, U. S. C. G., Master Mariner, Chief Deck Branch, U. S. Coast Guard Institute; Lieutenant Commander R. J. Lichtenberg, Master Mariner, U. S. Merchant Marine Academy; Lieutenant Commander W. J. Theroux, U. S. C. G., Nautical Science Department, Section Chief, Advanced Nautical Science, U. S. Coast Guard Academy.

The opinions or assertions contained herein, however, are our own and are not to be construed as official or reflecting the views of the Commandant or the Coast Guard at large.

B. A. Farnsworth

Larry C. Young

NAUTICAL RULES OF THE ROAD

INTRODUCTION

As this book enters its second decade, the third edition continues to provide a practical means for mariners and pleasure boaters to learn the indispensable Rules of the Road. In the late 1970s and early 1980s, mariners were faced with the task of learning to operate under the International Regulations for Preventing Collisions at Sea, 1972 (COLREGS) and the Inland Rules. Readers of the earlier editions—many of them seasoned sailors—had to unlearn many rules and change patterns to meet the new requirements. This mandated a section in the previous editions discussing the differences between the old and new regulations. A comparison section does not appear in this edition, but comments in the text may still refer to the "old" and "new" regulations.

The aim of this text is to make learning the Rules as easy as possible. To achieve this aim, on most pages the COLREGS are shown in the left-hand column and the Inland Rules in the right-hand column. Where the two sets of a particular Rule do not differ in content and meaning, the Rule is printed in a single centered column. Comments on the Rules are on the facing page.

With the publication of the Coast Guard "question bank," it is now possible to supply actual questions on examination subjects. Therefore, we have added in appendix A a section of Coast Guard examination questions on the Rules of the Road to help you understand what to expect on the Coast Guard test. This is not an attempt to offer all the possible questions. The Coast Guard has already issued a book that does this and it should be a good source text; however, the questions in this text will be helpful as a means of reinforcing the material presented.

This book does not include specific court cases, nor does it address every technicality that may arise. It is designed to provide a simple, straightforward presentation of the Rules that will be useful for all who need to learn and apply them.

Many people make the mistake of studying the Rules by beginning with Rule 1 and plodding through each Rule in hopes of being able to make some sense out of the total body of knowledge. In our view that is not the best way to garner a working knowledge of the Rules of the Road. Since learning is a building process, our method of study, outlined in appendix B to this book, defines the building blocks, beginning with the definitions upon which the Rules are based. All of the situations and maneuvers addressed in the Rules are based on proper application of these definitions.

After the definitions are in place, we can begin to apply them to particular situations; then the categories of vessels can be applied to the "pecking order" of those vessels listed in Rule 18. Next, we can relate them to actual maneuvering situations—meeting, crossing, or overtaking. We will already know about those situations if we have learned the definitions. Next, we can move on to responsibilities of the vessels involved in each of those situations. Having done so, we can add the dimension of restricted visibility and notice how those responsibilities change. After that, we can study the special conditions and requirements in the Rules, such as "not to impede" and "narrow channels." We can then add lights to the vessels, and notice that the situations will not change, but the manner of identifying them most certainly will. Night operations are very different from daylight maneuvers. Finally, after all else is mastered, we can go back to Rule 2 and discover certain conditions in which we might be required to take action other than that required by the Rules.

This outline for study is presented in response to many requests for ideas on the best way to approach instruction of the Rules. Instructors and individuals who are faced with the task of learning the Rules on their own should find it helpful.

We hope that all your crossing situations may have happy endings.

PART A
GENERAL

Rule 1. Application

(a) These Rules shall apply to all vessels upon the high seas and in all waters connected therewith navigable by seagoing vessels.

Rule 1. Application

(a) These Rules apply to all vessels upon the inland waters of the United States, and to vessels of the United States on the Canadian waters of the Great Lakes to the extent that there is no conflict with Canadian law.

(b) Nothing in these Rules shall interfere with the operation of special rules made by an appropriate authority for roadsteads, harbors, rivers, lakes or inland waterways connected with the high seas and navigable by seagoing vessels. Such special rules shall conform as closely as possible to these Rules.

(c) Nothing in these Rules shall interfere with the operation of any special rules made by the Government of any State

(b) *(i)* These Rules constitute special rules made by an appropriate authority within the meaning of Rule 1 (b) of the International Regulations.

(ii) All vessels complying with the construction and equipment requirements of the International Regulations are considered to be in compliance with these Rules.

(c) Nothing in these Rules shall interfere with the operation of any special rules made by the Secretary of the Navy

Rule 1.

(a) The International Rules (COLREGS) apply to vessels on the high seas and connecting waters. The Inland Rules apply to vessels navigating the inland waters of the United States. Defined by the COLREGS *demarcation lines*, set forth in 33 CFR (*Code of Federal Regulations*), Part 82, inland waters are drawn and identified on most United States charts. The Inland Rules also apply to United States vessels on "Canadian waters of the Great Lakes to the extent that there is no conflict with Canadian law." The Inland Rules became effective on the Great Lakes in March of 1983.

"Inland Waters," as the term is defined by the Rules of the Road, are not the same as "Inland Waters" for the purpose of Coast Guard licensing. For licensing purposes, any waters shoreward of the boundary line (as delineated in 46 CFR Part 7) are inland waters. Therefore, you must pass an examination on the COLREGS to be able to operate on all Inland Waters of the United States. Although this is a bit confusing, that's the way it is. Each set of regulations defines its own terms.

(b) The Inland Rules are made by "appropriate authority" as indicated by Rule 1 (b) of the COLREGS. They are written in the same type of format and, generally speaking, in the same order as the COLREGS— thus, Rule 3 of the Inland Rules will address the same subjects as Rule 3 of the COLREGS. This is a great boon to the student who can concentrate on the similarities of the two sets of Rules, rather than on the many differences.

(c) The Navy is allowed, by the Inland Rules, to make "special rules with respect to *additional* station or signal lights and shapes or whistle signals" for their vessels. For instance, the Navy presently plans to use strobe lights for daylight operation to indicate a vessel restricted in its

with respect to additional station or signal lights or whistle signals for ships of war and vessels proceeding under convoy, or with respect to additional station or signal lights for fishing vessels engaged in fishing as a fleet. These additional station or signal lights or whistle signals shall, so far as possible, be such that they cannot be mistaken for any light or signal authorized elsewhere under these Rules.

with respect to additional station or signal lights and shapes or whistle signals for ships of war and vessels proceeding under convoy, or by the Secretary with respect to additional station or signal lights and shapes for fishing vessels engaged in fishing as a fleet. These additional station or signal lights and shapes or whistle signals shall, so far as possible, be such that they cannot be mistaken for any light, shape, or signal authorized elsewhere under these Rules. Notice of such special rules shall be published in the Federal Register and, after the effective date specified in such notice, they shall have effect as if they were a part of these Rules.

(d) Traffic separation schemes may be adopted by the Organization for the purpose of these Rules.

(d) Vessel traffic service regulations may be in effect in certain areas.

(e) Whenever the Government concerned shall have determined that a vessel of special construction or purpose cannot comply fully with the provisions of any of these Rules with respect to the number, position, range or arc of visibility of lights or shapes, as well as to the disposition and

(e) Whenever the Secretary determines that a vessel or class of vessels of special construction or purpose cannot comply fully with the provisions of any of these Rules with respect to the number, position, range, or arc of visibility of lights or shapes, as well as to the disposition and characteristics of sound-signal-

ability to maneuver. These will actually be much more visible than the present day shapes, and will no doubt provide a better factor of safety, but will not be recognizable to a mariner with a passing knowledge of the Rules of the Road. There are also provisions regarding Rules for special lights for fishing vessels. These Rules are to be made by the secretary of the department in which the Coast Guard is operating. At the present time, this is the Secretary of Transportation.

(d) (International) For an explanation of Traffic Separation Schemes, see the comments on Rule 10.

(Inland) Vessel Traffic Service (VTS) regulations are in existence for certain ports in the United States. They will generally be explained by a note on current editions of charts for the affected area. Promulgated by the Coast Guard, the regulations differ from area to area, but they usually require, at least, that vessels monitor a certain radio channel or frequency and make periodic position reports to the Coast Guard's VTS head-quarters. A small booklet is published for each area, containing informa-tion and regulations for the use of that service.

(e) In this Rule authority is granted to allow vessels of special con-struction or purpose to be in less than full compliance with the Rules. However, these vessels must still comply as closely as possible and must be issued a certificate of alternative compliance. This is obtained from the Secretary of the Navy for naval vessels and from the Secretary of Transportation for all other vessels.

characteristics of sound-signalling appliances, such vessel shall comply with such other provisions in regard to the number, position, range or arc of visibility of lights or shapes, as well as to the disposition and characteristics of sound-signalling appliances, as her Government shall have determined to be the closest possible compliance with these Rules in respect of that vessel.

ling appliances, the vessel shall comply with such other provisions in regard to the number, position, range, or arc of visibility of lights or shapes, as well as to the disposition and characteristics of sound-signalling appliances, as the Secretary shall have determined to be the closest possible compliance with these Rules. The Secretary may issue a certificate of alternative compliance for a vessel or class of vessels specifying the closest possible compliance with these Rules. The Secretary of the Navy shall make these determinations and issue certificates of alternative compliance for vessels of the Navy.

(f) The Secretary may accept a certificate of alternative compliance issued by a contracting party to the International Regulations if he determines that the alternative compliance standards of the contracting party are substantially the same as those of the United States.

Rule 2. Responsibility

(a) Nothing in these Rules shall exonerate any vessel, or the owner, master or crew thereof, from the consequences of any neglect to comply with these Rules or of the neglect of any precaution which may be required by the ordinary practice of seamen, or by the special circumstances of the case.

Rule 2.

This Rule is the general catchall that applies when all others fail. The wording is the same in the COLREGS and the Inland Rules.

(a) Rule 2(a) is commonly known as the "Rule of Good Seamanship." It gets its name from the fact that it mandates "any precaution which may be required by the ordinary practice of seamen, or by the special circumstances of the case." Good seamanship includes, among other things:

(b) In construing and complying with these Rules due regard shall be had to all dangers of navigation and collision and to any special circumstances, including the limitations of the vessels involved, which may make a departure from these Rules necessary to avoid immediate danger.

Rule 3. General Definitions

For the purpose of these Rules, except where the context otherwise requires:

(a) The word "vessel" includes every description of water craft, including non-displacement craft and seaplanes, used or capable of being used as a means of transportation on water.

1. obeying the Rules of the Road
2. taking the best possible actions to avoid collision
3. taking action to lessen the effects of collision
4. using radiotelephone properly

Many things that historically have fallen in the area of good seamanship are now also specifically addressed in the Rules. A few examples are:

1. keeping a proper lookout—Rule 5
2. taking certain mandated actions to avoid collisions—Rule 8
3. showing of lights—Rule 20
4. using radar properly—Rules 6 (b) and 7 (b)

(b) Rule 2 (b) is known as the "General Prudential Rule." When the Rules do not cover a particular situation, this Rule becomes of paramount importance. The Rule is undoubtedly more often employed in inland waters than in international waters. For instance, a situation that involves more than two vessels has historically fallen under this Rule. Such situations will occur many more times in the congested inland waters than in international waters.

Rule 2 also covers the "in extremis case" and the situation when action contrary to the Rules is proposed by one vessel and accepted by another. The essential purpose of the Rule is to make it possible for vessels to take appropriate action in "special circumstances" to avoid "immediate danger." However, it does not mean that a vessel can take any action she deems expedient in any given situation. We need to be very careful not to use this Rule as an excuse for not knowing or complying with the other Rules. This Rule assumes that you know all the other rules and have decided that, for a very good defendable reason, they cannot be applied.

Rule 3.

This Rule gives the general definitions to be used in the Rules themselves. The definitions for lights are given in Rule 21 and those for whistle signals in Rule 32.

(a) The Rules of the Road apply to vessels, so this term is defined. We must be very careful of definitions and of how the Rules apply them and how the Coast Guard interprets them. For instance, while almost everything on the water is a vessel, there may be some exceptions. A barge may be used as a restaurant or band platform and not be required to show typical lights, depending on how she is moored. An exception that will become increasingly more common is the Mobile Offshore Drilling Unit (MODU), which must be lighted as a vessel while underway. Once

(b) The term "power-driven vessel" means any vessel propelled by machinery.

(c) The term "sailing vessel" means any vessel under sail provided that propelling machinery, if fitted, is not being used.

(d) The term "vessel engaged in fishing" means any vessel fishing with nets, lines, trawls or other fishing apparatus which restrict maneuverability, but does not include a vessel fishing with trolling lines or other fishing apparatus which do not restrict maneuverability.

(e) The word "seaplane" includes any aircraft designed to maneuver on the water.

(f) The term "vessel not under command" means a vessel which through some exceptional circumstances is unable to maneuver as required by these Rules and is therefore unable to keep out of the way of another vessel.

(g) The term "vessel restricted in her ability to maneuver" means a vessel which from the nature of her work is restricted in her ability to maneuver as required by these Rules and is therefore unable to keep out of the way of another vessel.

The term 'vessels restricted in their ability to maneuver' shall include but not be limited to:

(g) The term "vessel restricted in her ability to maneuver" means a vessel which from the nature of her work is restricted in her ability to maneuver as required by these Rules and is therefore unable to keep out of the way of another vessel; vessels restricted in their ability to maneuver include, but are not limited to:

the unit is attached to the Outer Continental Shelf for drilling, however, it is considered a fixed platform, and not a vessel, for the purposes of the Rules. It is interesting to note that the term "seaplane" is defined separately, but is included under the definition of the term "vessel." Therefore, any rule which addresses itself to a "vessel" applies to seaplanes as well, although Rule 18 (d) states: "A seaplane on the water shall, in general, keep well clear of all vessels."

(d) To be considered "engaged in fishing," a vessel must be using gear which restricts maneuverability. For this reason, most vessels fishing with lines, such as charter boats, are not considered engaged in fishing if they are trolling. If, however, the vessels are using trolling lines or gear long enough or deep enough to hamper their ability to comply with the Rules then they, too, would fall in this category. Should the fisherman be unfortunate enough to tangle with gear or steel other than his own, however, he would have to prove that he was deserving of the designation. He would also have to be showing proper lights or shapes for a vessel claiming such a privilege.

(f) You will note that the term "not under command" applies to vessels "which cannot maneuver due to some exceptional circumstance." That generally means that the qualifying circumstance is beyond the control of vessel personnel. A fisherman who decides to put up the "not under command" lights so he can leave the bridge and get some sleep is not keeping to the spirit of the Rules. In fact, he is breaking the law (Rule 5).

(g) In defining the term "vessel restricted in her ability to maneuver," the Rules are self-explanatory. Although a vessel that is "not under command" certainly has restricted maneuverability, she is not "restricted in her ability to maneuver" as defined by the Rules. A fishing vessel must be using gear which "restricts maneuverability" (Rule 3 (d)) in order to be considered a "vessel engaged in fishing," but this does not make her a "vessel restricted in her ability to maneuver" according to the Rules. These distinctions may seem minor but become important when applying Rule 18 (c) which states that a "vessel engaged in fishing when underway shall, so far as possible, keep out of the way of:
1. a vessel not under command;
2. a vessel restricted in her ability to maneuver."

(i) a vessel engaged in laying, servicing or picking up a navigation mark, submarine cable or pipeline;

(ii) a vessel engaged in dredging, surveying or underwater operations;

(iii) a vessel engaged in replenishment or transferring persons, provisions or cargo while underway;

(iv) a vessel engaged in the launching or recovery of aircraft;

(v) a vessel engaged in mineclearance operations; and

(vi) a vessel engaged in a towing operation such as severely restricts the towing vessel and her tow in their ability to deviate from their course.

(h) The term "vessel constrained by her draft" means a power-driven vessel which, because of her draft in relation to the available depth and width of navigable water, is severely restricted in her ability to deviate from the course she is following.

Both sets of Rules give a list of vessels that are "restricted in their ability to maneuver," but the Rules state that the vessels "include, but are not limited to" those in the list.

This may lead to a question about what additional vessels might be included in the list. It might also lead to a situation in which an operator decides that, due to the nature of his work, his vessel falls into this category. Any ideas of this nature should be discouraged. No one should take it upon himself to add things to the Rules, especially when it could create confusion and possible disaster. In case of a collision, the vessel involved would have the burden of proof that she was "restricted in her ability to maneuver" as defined by the Rules. However, this is not to declare decisively that the given list is exhaustive, but rather that one should think twice before deeming his ship to be in this category.

We should also point out at this juncture that Rule 3(g)(vi) states that vessels engaged in towing operations may be considered restricted in their ability to maneuver. The requirement for this designation is that their work must "severely restrict" them in their ability to make course changes. The Rule does not specify what type of towing is involved, thereby allowing the definition to apply to these vessels whether they are towing astern, alongside, or by pushing ahead.

(h) The International Maritime Organization (IMO), formerly known as IMCO, has published a clarification of the definition of a "vessel constrained by her draft" which reads as follows:

Not only the depth of water but also the available navigable water should be used as a factor to determine whether a vessel may be regarded as constrained by her draft. When determining this, due account should also be taken of the vessel and thus her ability to deviate from the course she is following. A vessel navigating in an area with a small under-keel clearance but with adequate space to take avoiding action should not be regarded as a vessel constrained by her draft.

The term "vessel constrained by her draft" is not included in the Inland Rules. Since the inland waters are more congested, it might be a great temptation for a vessel to consider herself "constrained by her draft" and perhaps to assume a right of way that is not hers. The International Rules direct vessels to "avoid impeding" a vessel constrained by her draft but do not give the constrained vessel the right of way. In congested waters, where several vessels are operating in a channel, this could become a very confusing situation.

(i) The word "underway" means that a vessel is not at anchor, or made fast to the shore, or aground.

(j) The words "length" and "breadth" of a vessel mean her length overall and greatest breadth.

(k) Vessels shall be deemed to be in sight of one another only when one can be observed visually from the other.

(l) The term "restricted visibility" means any condition in which visibility is restricted by fog, mist, falling snow, heavy rainstorms, sandstorms or any other similar causes.

(h) The word "underway" means that a vessel is not at anchor, or made fast to the shore, or aground;

(i) The words "length" and "breadth" of a vessel mean her length overall and greatest breadth;

(j) Vessels shall be deemed to be in sight of one another only when one can be observed visually from the other;

(k) The term "restricted visibility" means any condition in which visibility is restricted by fog, mist, falling snow, heavy rainstorms, sandstorms, or any other similar causes;

(l) "Western Rivers" means the Mississippi River, its tributaries, South Pass, and Southwest Pass, to the navigational demarcation lines dividing the high seas from harbors, rivers, and other inland waters of the United States, and the Port Allen-Morgan City Alternate Route, and that part of the Atchafalaya River above its junction with the Port Allen-Morgan City Alternate Route including the Old River and the Red River;

(m) "Great Lakes" means the Great Lakes and their connecting and tributary waters including the Calumet River as far as the Thomas J. O'Brien Lock and Controlling Works (between mile 326 and 327), the Chicago River as far as the east

(l) (Inland) The term "Western Rivers" is used in Rules 9 (a) *(ii)*, 15 (b) and 24 *(i)*, and includes the entire Mississippi River system south to the COLREGS demarcation lines.

(m) (Inland) The term "Great Lakes" is defined in this paragraph and is used in Rules 1 (a), 9 (a) *(ii)*, 15 (b), and 23 (d).

side of the Ashland Avenue
Bridge (between mile 321 and
322), and the Saint Lawrence
River as far east as the lower
exit of Saint Lambert Lock;

(n) "Secretary" means the
Secretary of the department in
which the Coast Guard is
operating;

(o) "Inland Waters" means
the navigable waters of the
United States shoreward of the
navigational demarcation lines
dividing the high seas from
harbors, rivers, and other inland waters of the United
States and the waters of the
Great Lakes on the United
States side of the International
Boundary;

(p) "Inland Rules" or "Rules"
mean the Inland Navigational
Rules and the annexes thereto,
which govern the conduct of vessels and specify the lights,
shapes, and sound signals that
apply on inland waters; and

(q) "International Regulations" means the International
Regulations for Preventing
Collisions at Sea, 1972, including annexes currently in force
for the United States.

(o) (inland) The term "Inland Waters" includes the Great Lakes (on the United States side of the boundary) and the Western Rivers for the purposes of these Rules. Where exceptions are made for these waters, as in Rule 15 (b), they are specifically stated.

PART B
STEERING AND SAILING RULES

I

CONDUCT OF VESSELS
IN ANY CONDITION OF VISIBILITY

Rule 4. Application

Rules in this section apply to any condition of visibility.

Rule 4. Application

Rules in this subpart apply in any condition of visibility.

Rule 5. Look-out

Every vessel shall at all times maintain a proper look-out by sight and hearing as well as by all available means appropriate in the prevailing circumstances and conditions so as to make a full appraisal of the situation and of the risk of collision.

Rule 4.

There are three sections (international) or subparts (Inland) to the Steering and Sailing Rules. Section (Subpart) I of Part B applies to "any condition of visibility" and includes Rules 4 through 10. These Rules must be followed *at all times*. Section (Subpart) II includes Rules 11 through 18 and applies to vessels "in sight of one another." Section (Subpart) III applies to vessels in "restricted visibility" and is comprised of Rule 19.

Rule 5.

This Rule gives instructions about the responsibilities of a vessel with regard to keeping a "proper lookout" which is to be done by:
1. sight
2. sound (hearing)
3. all available means appropriate

The mariner is responsible for taking all available means appropriate to determine the presence and location of other vessels. The IMO (International Maritime Organization) Recommendations on Navigational Watch-keeping, which provide more guidance in this area, state that keeping a look-out involves making "a full appraisal of the situation, and of the risk of collision, stranding and other hazards to navigation." The duties of a look-out also include "the detection of ships or aircraft in distress, shipwrecked persons, wrecks and debris." The task of a look-out is not something to be taken lightly. All his energies must be devoted to the job. For this reason the IMO recommendations state that:
1. No duties shall be assigned or undertaken which would interfere with the keeping of a proper look-out;

Rule 6. Safe Speed

Every vessel shall at all times proceed at a safe speed so that she can take proper and effective action to avoid collision and be stopped within a distance appropriate to the prevailing circumstances and conditions.

In determining a safe speed the following factors shall be among those taken into account:

(a) By all vessels:

(i) the state of visibility;

(ii) the traffic density including concentrations of fishing vessels or any other vessels;

(iii) the maneuverability of the vessel with special reference to stopping distance and turning ability in the prevailing conditions;

(iv) at night the presence of background light such as from shore lights and from back scatter of her own lights;

(v) the state of wind, sea, and current, and the proximity of navigational hazards;

(vi) the draft in relation to the available depth of water.

2. The duties of the look-out and helmsman are separate, and a helmsman who is steering is not a look-out;

3. During the day, there may be circumstances in which the officer of the watch can safely be the sole look-out, but only after he assesses each situation. Even then, IMO states, "assistance must be immediately available."

It is advisable to have the look-out separate from the bridge watch, and as close to the bow as possible. If the look-out is low in the vessel and close to the water, rather than aloft, he can also get a better sense of the direction of fog signals. Such a position will, as well, remove him from the distracting noises of diesel engines and other machinery.

Rule 6.

The location of this Rule in Section (Subpart) I of the Steering and Sailing Rules indicates that the Rule applies in any condition of visibility. The Rule states that vessels "shall *at all times* proceed at a safe speed." At midnight or noon, in fair weather or fog, a vessel must be operated at a safe speed. Safe speed includes those factors of safety affecting your vessel as well as other vessels or structures in its vicinity. As far as she is concerned, a VLCC (very large crude carrier) may be able to operate safely at a speed of 15 knots, but if she is operating in restricted or congested waters, she may be a hazard to smaller vessels, or to piers and other shore structures. Even the wake of relatively small vessels may cause a good deal of damage to small anchored vessels, vessels in crowded waters, or vessels tied up at a marina. In most cases, vessel operators are held liable for damages caused by their wake. So although the state of visibility is the first thing most mariners think of which affects safe speed, there are other things to be considered. The Rule lists them as well as factors to be considered by vessels using radar.

The last point made in the Rule pertains to the use of radar. A vessel might well be able to determine precisely the distance of visibility by noting the distance shown by radar at the time of visual sighting of the object. There will also be instances, especially at night, when a strong radar target is picked up, but cannot be sighted visually. This will notify the watch officer that visibility is restricted (perhaps more so than he had thought), and that closer attention to lookout duties, and perhaps a change in the vessel's speed, is in order. By using the radar to its full capacity and knowing the maneuvering characteristics of his vessel, the ship's officer can make a better assessment of what is a safe speed than

(b) Additionally, by vessels with operational radar:

(i) the characteristics, efficiency and limitations of the radar equipment;

(ii) any constraints imposed by the radar range scale in use;

(iii) the effect on radar detection of the sea state, weather and other sources of interference;

(iv) the possibility that small vessels, ice and other floating objects may not be detected by radar at an adequate range;

(v) the number, location and movement of vessels detected by radar;

(vi) the more exact assessment of the visibility that may be possible when radar is used to determine the range of vessels or other objects in the vicinity.

Rule 7. Risk of Collision

(a) Every vessel shall use all available means appropriate to the prevailing circumstances and conditions to determine if risk of collision exists. If there is any doubt such risk shall be deemed to exist.

(b) Proper use shall be made of radar equipment if fitted and operational, including long-range scanning to obtain early warning of risk of collision and radar plotting or equivalent systematic observation of detected objects.

(c) Assumptions shall not be made on the basis of scanty information, especially scanty radar information.

(d) In determining if risk of collision exists the following considerations shall be among those taken into account:

(i) such risk shall be deemed to exist if the compass bearing of an approaching

an officer on a vessel that is not radar-equipped. In short, radar is not a tool to be used as an excuse for high speed in conditions restricting visibility.

Rule 7.

Since actions to be taken by vessels according to the Rules are usually predicated upon the fact that risk of collision exists, we must have suitable methods for determining whether the required condition is met. When vessels are crossing, the vessel which has the other on her own starboard side must keep out of the way if the circumstances are such "as to involve risk of collision" (Rule 15).

Rule 17 (Action by Stand-on Vessel) is to be complied with "where one of two vessels is to keep out of the way." This means that a situation must exist and, therefore, risk of collision must exist, for the Rule to apply. Rule 14 applies when vessels are meeting "so as to involve risk of collision." Therefore, we must have a good understanding of risk of collision before we can apply these Rules.

Paragraph (a) and (b) of Rule 7 tell us that we are bound to use all means at our disposal to determine if risk of collision exists. Paragraph (d) tells us that risk of collision does exist if the compass bearing of an approaching vessel does not change appreciably. This would be a good time to explain the fact that the Rules use the term "approaching" as a relative term. There is no requirement for both vessels to be making way for risk of collision to exist, and, if it exists for one vessel, it surely exists

vessel does not appreciably change;

(ii) such risk may sometimes exist even when an appreciable bearing change is evident, particularly when approaching a very large vessel or a tow or when approaching a vessel at close range.

Rule 8. Action to Avoid Collision

(a) Any action taken to avoid collision shall, if the circumstances of the case admit, be positive, made in ample time and with due regard to the observance of good seamanship.

for the other one. To argue that, since the other guy was not "approaching," there was no risk of collision, will not greatly influence an investigator who happens to be taking pictures of the "unapproaching" vessel's anchor in your hawsepipe. So we must conclude that when two vessels are getting closer together each minute, they should each view the other as an "approaching" vessel, despite that vessel's true course and speed. The same paragraph also tells us that risk of collision may exist even when the compass bearing is changing. We must use radar to assist us in making our determination (paragraph (b)), but we must not make any assumptions based on scanty radar information (paragraph (c)).

The question still remains, "At what point does the risk of collision exist?" We cannot define it merely by distance, for certainly two supertankers approaching each other on constant bearings would reach the point of risk sooner than two pleasure yachts on the same courses. The simple fact is that often, the time when "risk of collision" occurs is determined by the court after the collision occurred. Perhaps as a general rule, we could say that risk of collision exists at the point in time when a maneuver contrary to any of the Rules will result in the danger of collision, either by the maneuver alone or by the interpretation of that maneuver by the other vessel.

Rule 8.

This Rule gives guidelines for any action to be taken in accordance with the Rules, and should be applied in conjunction with, and not separate from, the other Rules for conduct of vessels. Rule 8 does not give a stand-on vessel the right to take early action to avoid a situation; such action is covered by Rule 17.

(a) If the circumstances of the case admit, the action must be "positive" and made "in ample time." If in congested waters or narrow channels, the circumstances may be such that a vessel might not be able to take action as positively or as early as would otherwise be required. Remember that this Rule applies in any condition of visibility. Rule 16 requires a give-way vessel to take early action to keep clear of the stand-on vessel when the vessels are in sight. Rule 19 (d) requires any vessel in restricted visibility to take action in "ample time" if she detects another vessel by radar and determines that a close-quarters situation is developing. A stand-on vessel may take action only after she determines that the give-way vessel is not taking appropriate action (Rule 17 (a) *(ii)*, and so the circumstances of the case may not permit her to comply with the "ample time" requirement.

(b) Any alteration of course and/or speed to avoid collision shall, if the circumstances of the case admit, be large enough to be readily apparent to another vessel observing visually or by radar; a succession of small alterations of course and/or speed should be avoided.

(b) Any alteration of course or speed to avoid collision shall, if the circumstances of the case admit, be large enough to be readily apparent to another vessel observing visually or by radar; a succession of small alterations of course or speed should be avoided.

(c) If there is sufficient sea room, alteration of course alone may be the most effective action to avoid a close-quarters situation provided that it is made in good time, is substantial and does not result in another close-quarters situation.

(b) This paragraph provides guidelines to use when taking action to avoid collision. It is important that the other vessel in the situation be able to tell what your vessel is doing. If your vessel is the give-way vessel, your evasive action should be such that the stand-on vessel will be certain that you are taking appropriate action. Otherwise, she may take action that, although not contrary to the rules, may certainly confuse the situation and make your task of keeping clear more difficult.

In restricted visibility, it is especially important to make any course changes substantial. If you make a series of small course changes and another vessel is plotting you on radar, your relative motion line may appear as if you are on a steady course. (See figure below)

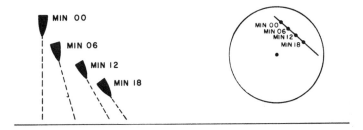

A substantial course change would let the other vessel know that you are definitely taking action. (See figure below)

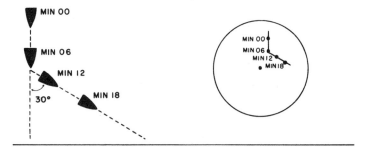

In clear visibility it would be advisable, if at all possible, to make the course change substantial enough to change the aspect of the vessel from the observer's viewpoint, that is, to show him the opposite bow during daylight, or the opposite sidelight at night.

(c) An alteration of course may be the most effective action because

1. It can generally be done faster than a change in speed;

2. It will change the aspect of the vessel in relation to an observer, thus letting him know that action is being taken. A change of speed may not accomplish this.

(d) Action taken to avoid collision
with another vessel shall be such as to
result in passing at a safe distance. The
effectiveness of the action shall be care-
fully checked until the other vessel is finally past and clear.

(e) If necessary to avoid collision or
allow more time to assess the situation, a
vessel shall slacken her speed or take all
way off by stopping or reversing her
means of propulsion.

(f) *(i)* A vessel which, by any of these
rules, is required not to impede the passage or safe passage of another vessel
shall, when required by the circumstances
of the case, take early action to allow sufficient sea room for the safe passage of the
other vessel.

(ii) A vessel required not to impede
the passage or safe passage of another vessel is not relieved of this obligation if approaching the other vessel so as to involve
risk of collision and shall, when taking action, have full regard to the action which
may be required by the rules of this part.

(iii) A vessel the passage of which is
not to be impeded remains fully obliged to
comply with the rules of this part when
the two vessels are approaching one
another so as to involve risk of collision.

3. It will generally change the relative motion line on an observing vessel's radar faster than a change of speed.

(d) The vessel taking action in accordance with this Rule is responsible for checking the effectiveness of the action and making certain the other vessel is "past and clear." A workable definition of "past and clear" would be that point at which:

1. The vessels are a suitable distance apart for the conditions, and

2. Any reasonable maneuver by either vessel would not create another situation involving risk of collision between those two vessels.

(e) When operating in restricted waters, a change of course great enough to avoid collision may be out of the question. In this case, a change of speed is mandatory. The Rules do not prohibit an increase in speed to avoid collision, but the general tone of the Rules is to favor speed reductions. A vessel must at all times proceed at a "safe speed," and therefore, a vessel's authority to increase speed is limited by Rule 6. Also, since this Rule applies in any condition of visibility, we must use it in conjunction with the other Rules for operating in that condition. See Rules 5, 6, and 19.

(f) There are several rules which dictate to certain vessels that they are not to "impede" other vessels. This Rule was added as an amendment to the Rules in 1989. The term has had a rather difficult time gaining acceptance and has managed to defy logical explanation. Yet, it is necessary because of differences in vessels' size, speed, draft, maneuvering characteristics, occupation, and because of a variety of other reasons.

Vessels that are directed "not to impede" other vessels are addressed in Rules 8, 9, 10, and 18. The writers of the Rules did not want them to be contradictory with respect to the right-of-way. When a Rule states that a vessel is to "keep out of the way," that means the other vessel in the situation has the "right-of-way." Right-of-way is based upon vessel *location* with respect to the other vessel [See Rules 9(a)*(ii)*, 12, 13, 14(d), 15, and 17(d)], or in some cases its *definition* (Rule 18).

Sometimes, however, location or definition alone is not an adequate indicator of who has or shares the responsibility for avoiding collision. What if the "give-way" vessel is not easily maneuvered, or is operating in a channel where her draft may not allow her to make the course changes ordinarily required by her duty as a "give-way" vessel?

If a loaded tanker proceeds down a channel, and a sailing vessel is crossing ahead from starboard to port, who has the right-of-way? The sailing vessel has. But at the same time the sailing vessel is directed "not

Rule 9. Narrow Channels

(a) A vessel proceeding along the course of a narrow channel or fairway shall keep as near to the outer limit of the channel or fairway which lies on her starboard side as is safe and practicable.

Rule 9. Narrow Channels

(a) *(i)* A vessel proceeding along the course of a narrow channel or fairway shall keep as near to the outer limit of the channel or fairway which lies on her starboard side as is safe and practicable.

(ii) Notwithstanding paragraph (a) *(i)* and Rule 14 (a), a power-driven vessel operating in narrow channels or fairways on the Great Lakes, Western Rivers, or waters specified by the Secretary, and proceeding downbound with a following current shall have the right-of-way over an upbound vessel, shall propose the manner and place of passage, and shall initiate the maneuvering signals prescribed by Rule 34 (a) (*i*), as appropriate. The vessel proceeding upbound against the current shall hold as necessary to permit safe passing.

(b) A vessel of less than 20 meters in length or a sailing vessel shall not impede the passage of a vessel which can

to impede" the passage of the tanker. The Rule recognizes the fact that small vessels have an easier time maneuvering in such a situation and places upon them a requirement to stay clear of the vessel within the channel. If collision occurred, and it was determined that one of the vessels (in this case the sailing vessel) could operate safely outside the channel, that vessel would most likely be held at fault. However, the Rule does not change the status of a give-way vessel to that of a stand-on vessel within the meaning of the Rules. (See further discussion of this term in Rule 9.)

Rule 9.

Paragraph (a) *(ii)* (Inland) grants the right-of-way to vessels with a following current when operating on the "Great Lakes, Western Rivers, or waters specified by the Secretary." However, with the right-of-way comes the responsibility for proposing the manner and place of passage, and for initiating the maneuvering signals required by Rule 34 (a) *(i)*. The responsibility for a safe passage, then, rests with the vessel which has the right-of-way—certainly an unusual circumstance.

Rule 9 puts the term "not to impede," to which we were just introduced in Rule 8, into actual practice in a situation. This is the first time we meet the term, but it will not be the last.

We may tend to think this Rule applies only to small vessels, but paragraphs (c) and (d) do not mention vessel size. It is conceivable in this day of the 60-to-70-foot mean draft that a 600-foot freighter with a draft of 35 feet might well find herself in the position of the vessel which, although having the right-of-way, is directed not to impede the other vessel. In international waters, the constrained vessel might well be showing signals for a "vessel constrained by her draft," thereby letting others know of her condition. In inland waters, however, there is no designation, "constrained by her draft." Therefore, it is imperative that watch officers keep a close eye on the characteristics and movements of other vessels in the vicinity.

It is interesting to note that under International Rules the danger signal is optional (Rule 9 (d)) for the vessel in the channel, and under Inland Rules it is mandatory.

There are no special whistle signals in the Inland Rules for overtaking in narrow channels when the overtaken vessel has to take action to facilitate passage. The Rule does not prevent the overtaken vessel from taking such action, but neither does it require her to do so. It does seem

safely navigate only within a narrow channel or fairway.

(c) A vessel engaged in fishing shall not impede the passage of any other vessel navigating within a narrow channel or fairway.

(d) A vessel shall not cross a narrow channel or fairway if such crossing impedes the passage of a vessel which can safely navigate only within such channel or fairway. The latter vessel may use the sound signal prescribed in Rule 34 (d) if in doubt as to the intention of the crossing vessel.

(e) *(i)* In a narrow channel or fairway when overtaking can take place only if the vessel to be overtaken has to take action to permit safe passing, the vessel intending to overtake shall indicate her intention by sounding the appropriate signal prescribed in Rule 34 (c) *(i)*. The vessel to be overtaken shall, if in agreement, sound the appropriate signal prescribed in Rule 34 (c) *(ii)* and take steps to permit safe passing. If in doubt she may sound the signals prescribed in Rule 34 (d).

(d) A vessel shall not cross a narrow channel or fairway if such crossing impedes the passage of a vessel which can safely navigate only within such channel or fairway. The latter vessel shall use the danger signal prescribed in Rule 34 (d) if in doubt as to the intention of the crossing vessel.

(e) *(i)* In a narrow channel or fairway when overtaking, the vessel intending to overtake shall indicate her intention by sounding the appropriate signal prescribed in Rule 34 (c) and take steps to permit safe passing. The overtaken vessel, if in agreement, shall sound the same signal. If in doubt she shall sound the danger signal prescribed in Rule 34 (d).

(ii) This Rule does not relieve the overtaking vessel of her obligation under Rule 13.

(f) A vessel nearing a bend or an area of a narrow channel or fairway where other vessels may be obscured by an intervening obstruction shall navigate with particular alertness and caution and

logical, however, that if she agrees to being passed, she accepts some of the responsibility for assuring a safe passage.

It should be noted that even though this Rule applies in any condition of visibility, the prescribed whistle signals shall be sounded *only* when the vessels are in sight of one another. (See the discussion of the whistle signals under Rule 34.)

9 (e) *(i)* (International) See discussion of this situation on page 115.

(Inland) Since this Rule refers to the signals prescribed in Rule 34(c), which may be sounded only by power-driven vessels, we must assume that this Rule also applies only to power-driven vessels.

Remembering that this Rule only applies to narrow channels or fairways, we should point out that agreement must be reached before the overtaking maneuver can be completed. Both vessels must sound whistle signals. Each vessel must be certain that the other agrees with the maneuver. If the vessel being overtaken responds to the overtures of the overtaking vessel with the danger/doubt signal, the overtaking vessel should hold back and not attempt to pass. It may be that the lead vessel wishes to be passed on the opposite side, or it may be that she considers any overtaking situation dangerous for the time being. Since signals should be initiated by the overtaking vessel in this situation, that vessel may try again. She may sound the same signal as before and hope for a favorable response, or she may indicate an intention to pass on the opposite side. Again, she must have permission before proceeding with the maneuver.

We will, in passing, mention the term "cross-signals." Although this term is not found in the Rules, it has come to mean a situation in which the answering vessel gives the opposite signal to that of the initiating vessel. Just because there is no allowance for such signals in the Rules does not mean they will never take place.

In the situation in Rule 9, cross-signals should be very unlikely in international waters, because the answering signal is completely dif-

shall sound the appropriate signal
prescribed in Rule 34 (e).

(g) Any vessel shall, if the circumstances of the case admit, avoid anchoring in a narrow channel.

(g) Every vessel shall, if the circumstances of the case admit, avoid anchoring in a narrow channel.

Rule 10. Traffic Separation Schemes

Rule 10. Vessel Traffic Services

Each vessel required by regulation to participate in a vessel traffic service shall comply with the applicable regulations.

(a) This rule applies to traffic separation schemes adopted by the Organization and does not relieve any vessel of her obligation under any other rule.

(b) A vessel using a traffic separation scheme shall:

(i) proceed in the appropriate traffic lane in the general direction of traffic flow for that lane;

ferent from the initiating signal. The vessel being overtaken can either answer the proposal with one prolonged, one short, one prolonged, and one short (— . — .) blast, or with the danger signal. If she answers with any other kind of signal, the overtaking vessel had better stay clear because it reflects a serious lack of knowledge of the Rules.

In inland waters, the overtaken vessel is supposed to answer, if in agreement, with "a similar sound signal." That means *exactly* the same. If she answers one blast with two blasts, that is a cross-signal, is confusing, illegal, and doesn't mean anything. The overtaking vessel cannot assume that the lead vessel is suggesting passing on the other side. She may just have made a mistake. The overtaking vessel should hold back, wait a bit, and try initiating another signal. This process must go on until a signal has been *initiated* by the overtaking vessel and *answered* by the same signal from the vessel being overtaken. The overtaking vessel is the one still responsible for the success of the maneuver (Rule 13).

Rule 10.

As each VTS (Vessel Traffic Service) is placed in operation, regulations for its use are published. Rule 10 (Inland) requires vessels to comply with the published regulations in order to be considered in compliance with the Rules of the Road. This gives VTS regulations an additional measure of authority over the shipping involved, and vessel personnel would be well advised to pay careful attention to the requirements of the Service in which they are operating.

Rule 10 (International) gives some directives for vessels that are operating in or near a traffic separation scheme. A watch officer should be sure that he understands the terms used in the Rule. IMO gives us a helping hand by defining the following terms in Resolution A. 284 *(viii)*:

(a) Traffic Separation Scheme—A scheme which separates traffic proceeding in opposite or nearly opposite directions by the use of a separation zone or line, traffic lanes, or by other means.

(b) Traffic Lane—An area within definite limits inside which one-way traffic is established.

(ii) so far as practicable keep clear of a traffic separation line or separation zone;

(iii) normally join or leave a traffic lane at the termination of the lane, but when joining or leaving from the side shall do so at as small an angle to the general direction of traffic flow as practicable.

(c) A vessel shall, so far as practicable, avoid crossing traffic lanes but if obliged to do so shall cross on a heading as nearly as practicable at right angles to the general direction of traffic flow.

(d) Inshore traffic zones shall not normally be used by through traffic which can safely use the appropriate traffic lane within the adjacent traffic separation scheme. However, vessels of less than 20 meters in length and sailing vessels may under all circumstances use inshore traffic zones.

(e) A vessel other than a crossing vessel or a vessel joining or leaving a lane shall not normally enter a separation zone or cross a separation line except:

(i) in cases of emergency to avoid immediate danger;

(ii) to engage in fishing within a separation zone.

(f) A vessel navigating in areas near the terminations of traffic separation schemes shall do so with particular caution.

(c) Separation Zone or Line—A zone or line separating traffic proceeding in one direction from traffic proceeding in another direction. A separation zone may also be used to separate a traffic lane from the adjacent inshore traffic zone.

(d) Inshore Traffic Zone-A designated area between the landward boundary of a traffic separation scheme and the adjacent coast intended for coastal traffic.

IMO has stated, as a clarification of paragraph (d), that vessels of less than 20 meters in length, or sailing vessels, may use the inshore zones even if they are through traffic.

Basically, when in the area of a traffic separation scheme, a vessel should either use the scheme or avoid it "by as wide a margin as possible" (Rule 10 (h)). This policy will save the consequences of any confusion resulting when applying the more vaguely worded parts of the Rule.

Vessels are allowed to engage in fishing in traffic separation schemes. However, they must:

1. proceed in the general direction of traffic flow, if fishing in a traffic lane; and

2. not impede the passage of any vessel following a traffic lane.

(g) A vessel shall so far as practicable avoid anchoring in a traffic separation scheme or in areas near its terminations.

(h) A vessel not using a traffic separation scheme shall avoid it by as wide a margin as is practicable.

(i) A vessel engaged in fishing shall not impede the passage of any vessel following a traffic lane.

(j) A vessel of less than 20 meters in length or a sailing vessel shall not impede the safe passage of a power-driven vessel following a traffic lane.

(k) A vessel restricted in her ability to maneuver when engaged in an operation for the maintenance of safety of navigation in a traffic separation scheme is exempted from complying with this Rule to the extent necessary to carry out the operation.

(l) A vessel restricted in her ability to maneuver when engaged in an operation for the laying, servicing or picking up of a submarine cable, within a traffic separation scheme, is exempted from complying with this Rule to the extent necessary to carry out the operation.

Again, we have a situation where the fishing vessel is directed "not to impede" the passage of other vessels. This obligation to stay clear would include the vessel and any working gear that may be extending from her. Thus the standard fishing-vessel claim that a merchant vessel ruined its gear would probably be nullified if the vessel were fishing in a traffic separation scheme. Fishermen should take great pains to ascertain their position correctly when operating in areas around the schemes.

See discussion of the "not to impede" situation in Rule 8 (f).

I I

CONDUCT OF VESSELS
IN SIGHT OF ONE ANOTHER

Rule 11. Application

Rules in this section apply to vessels in sight of one another.

Rule 11. Application

Rules in this subpart apply to vessels in sight of one another.

Rule 12. Sailing Vessels

(a) When two sailing vessels are approaching one another, so as to involve risk of collision, one of them shall keep out of the way of the other as follows:

(*i*) when each has the wind on a different side, the vessel which has the wind on the port side shall keep out of the way of the other;

(*ii*) when both have the wind on the same side, the vessel which is to windward shall keep out of the way of the vessel which is to leeward;

(*iii*) if a vessel with the wind on the port side sees a vessel to windward and cannot determine with certainty whether the other vessel has the wind on the port or on the starboard side, she shall keep out of the way of the other.

(b) For the purposes of this Rule the windward side shall be deemed to be the

Rule 11.

Rules 11-18 apply when vessels are "in sight of one another." Remember that this term is defined in Rule 3 (k) as existing "only when one can be observed visually from the other." A radar contact is not a visual contact.

Rule 12.

We will risk an oversimplification at this point in the interest of those who are unfamiliar with sail terminology. A vessel that has the wind on the port side, forward of the beam, will be carrying her largest fore-and-aft sail on the starboard side, and is on a *port tack*. A vessel that has the wind on the starboard side, forward of the beam, will be carrying her largest fore-and-aft sail on the port side, and is on a *starboard tack*. Thus, when two sail vessels are approaching, the vessel on the port tack must keep clear of the vessel on the starboard tack. In addition, the Rules no longer mention vessels having the wind abaft the beam, but only mention the side of the vessel on which the wind is blowing, so that a vessel with the wind forward of the beam on her port side must keep clear of a vessel with the wind abaft the beam on her starboard side.

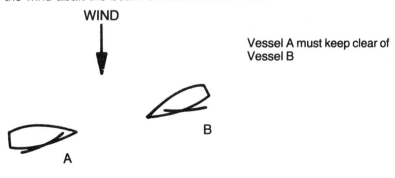

WIND

Vessel A must keep clear of
Vessel B

B

A

side opposite to that on which the main-
sail is carried or, in the case of a square-
rigged vessel, the side opposite to that on
which the largest fore-and-aft sail is
carried.

Rule 13. Overtaking

(a) Notwithstanding any-
thing contained in the Rules of
Part B, Sections I and II any
vessel overtaking any other
shall keep out of the way of the
vessel being overtaken.

Rule 13. Overtaking

(a) Notwithstanding any-
thing contained in Rules 4
through 18, any vessel overtaking any other shall keep out of
the way of the vessel being overtaken.

(b) A vessel shall be deemed to be overtaking when coming up with another vessel from a direction more than 22.5

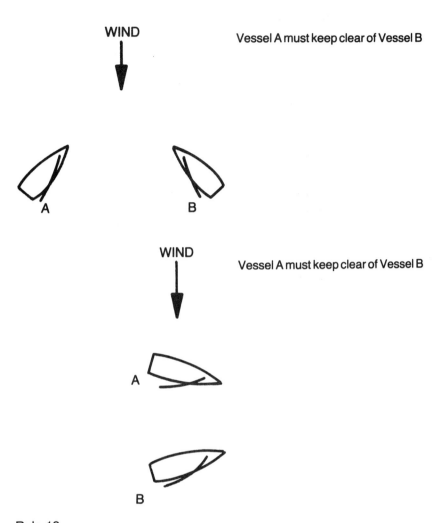

WIND

Vessel A must keep clear of Vessel B

A   B

WIND

Vessel A must keep clear of Vessel B

A

B

Rule 13.

Rule 13 applies to overtaking situations regardless of the conditions or characteristics of the vessels involved. It takes precedence over any other Rules in the section (subpart). An overtaking vessel "shall" keep out of the way of the vessel she is overtaking.

An overtaking situation exists when a vessel is approaching another from a direction more than 22.5 degrees abaft the beam. The Rule further explains that, at night, the overtaking vessel would be able to see only the sternlights of the vessel being overtaken. If a vessel can see either of the sidelights of a vessel she is approaching, an overtaking situation

degrees abaft her beam, that is, in such a position with reference to the vessel she is overtaking, that at night she would be able to see only the sternlight of that vessel but neither of her sidelights.

(c) When a vessel is in any doubt as to whether she is overtaking another, she shall assume that this is the case and act accordingly.

(d) Any subsequent alteration of the bearing between the two vessels shall not make the overtaking vessel a crossing vessel within the meaning of these Rules or relieve her of the duty of keeping clear of the overtaken vessel until she is finally past and clear.

does not exist. Since the situation seems rather well defined at night, paragraph (c) should apply mainly during daylight hours when the relative bearing would be more difficult to determine. If any doubt exists on the part of the overtaking vessel, she shall assume that an overtaking situation exists and keep out of the way.

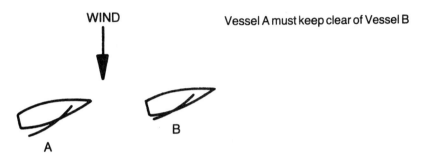

WIND

Vessel A must keep clear of Vessel B

A   B

Probably the first question that comes to the mind of the watch officer of the overtaking vessel in one of these situations is "what kind of situation do the personnel on the other vessel think is involved?" Perhaps the use of bridge-to-bridge radiotelephone communications could solve the problem. Such action is encouraged by the Inland Rules (see discussion of Rule 34 (h)) which require an agreement to be reached if passing within one-half mile. If this does not work, the situation deserves very careful attention. Assume that two vessels are approaching each other, during the day, as shown in the diagram below:

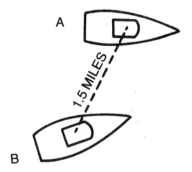

A

1.5 MILES

B

Let us assume that you are the watch officer on Vessel B. You are not sure whether you are approaching from more than 22.5 degrees abaft the beam. You then apply Rule 13 (c) and assume you are the overtaking vessel. If the Captain does not wish to be disturbed (or if you are the Captain), you must decide what to do.

For a moment, let us analyze the other vessel (Vessel A). If Vessel A also believes that an overtaking situation exists, she should hold course and speed. All will be well, and any proper avoiding action you take will succeed. Vessel A may even decide to help you realize that you are an overtaking vessel by applying just a few degrees of left rudder—not enough to deem it necessary to sound a whistle signal. (This action is not precisely legal, but you will undoubtedly encounter it from time to time.) But what if Vessel A decides that a crossing situation exists? In that case, she would be the give-way vessel and is directed to avoid crossing ahead of you (Rule 15). She may do this by slowing down or changing course to port. You may hope she would not change course to starboard since such a maneuver could not be easily defined as keeping "well clear" (Rule 16).

Now the question is what is the best action for you to take. The alternatives for Vessel A are:

1. hold course and speed (or perhaps change course slightly to the port)

2. slow down or stop

3. change course to port

The alternatives for Vessel B are:

1. hold course and speed

2. slow down or stop

3. change course to starboard

We have already stated that you (the watch officer on Vessel B) are in doubt as to whether it is a crossing or an overtaking situation. Even if convinced it is a crossing situation, you may still be required to take action (Rule 17). Therefore, it would seem prudent to rule out choice 1. Choice 2 is possible, and may be the best course of action in restricted or congested waters (Rule 8 (e)). The Rules state, however, that change of course is often the best solution (Rule 8 (c)), if there is sufficient sea room. You can see that no matter which alternative Vessel A chooses, a change of course to starboard for your vessel should result in a safer passing distance. Also, if you change course to starboard, you will sound a short blast on the whistle (international waters) thereby letting Vessel A know what you are doing (Rule 34 (a)). There is no sound signal for slowing down. The only signal available in that instance would be the danger signal (Rule 34 (d)) which might, or might not, produce a satisfactory solution to the problem (see discussion of required whistle signals under Rules 34-35).

Rule 14. Head-on Situation

(a) When two power-driven vessels are meeting on reciprocal or nearly reciprocal courses so as to involve risk of collision each shall alter her course to starboard so that each shall pass on the port side of the other.

(b) Such a situation shall be deemed to exist when a vessel sees the other ahead or nearly ahead and by night she could see the masthead lights of the other in a line or nearly in a line and/or both sidelights and by day she observes the corresponding aspect of the other vessel.

Rule 14. Head-on Situation

(a) Unless otherwise agreed, when two power-driven vessels are meeting on reciprocal or nearly reciprocal courses so as to involve risk of collision each shall alter her course to starboard so that each shall pass on the port side of the other.

(b) Such a situation shall be deemed to exist when a vessel sees the other ahead or nearly ahead and by night she could see the masthead lights of the other in a line or nearly in a line or both sidelights and by day she observes the corresponding aspect of the other vessel.

(c) When a vessel is in any doubt as to whether such a situation exists she shall assume that it does exist and act accordingly.

(d) Notwithstanding paragraph (a) of this Rule, a power-driven vessel operating on the Great Lakes, Western Rivers, or waters specified by the Secretary, and proceeding downbound with a following

Rule 13 (d) states that an overtaking vessel cannot become a crossing vessel once a situation has been established. The reason for this is that an overtaking vessel might change her status from give-way to stand-on. The Rules do not, however, prohibit a crossing vessel from becoming an overtaking vessel, since such an action would increase the vessel's burden by making her the give-way vessel.

In an overtaking situation involving two sailing vessels, the vessel overtaking the other must keep out of the way, since Rule 13 (a) supersedes all the other Rules in this section (subpart).

Rule 14.

For this Rule to apply the following conditions must exist:
1. Both vessels must be power-driven.
2. They must be meeting on reciprocal or nearly reciprocal courses.
3. The situation must involve risk of collision.

Risk of collision is defined in Rule 7. If the two vessels involved are far enough apart so that there is no risk of collision, this Rule will not apply. If it appears that they would pass dangerously close, however, each is directed to alter course to starboard. This requirement applies even when each vessel is on the other's starboard bow at the time risk of collision is determined.

Another requirement for the situation to exist is that a vessel must be able to see the other vessel's masts in a line, or both her sidelights. When this requirement is coupled with the reciprocal course requirement, it becomes obvious this is a very restrictive situation. Since sidelights cannot usually be seen more than about two degrees across each bow, a vessel seeing both sidelights at an angle of more than three or four degrees on either bow should determine that she is not involved in a head-on situation. A vessel seeing only a single sidelight dead ahead should come to the same conclusion.

The one circumstance that can lead to confusion in a head-on situation is that which involves a vessel or vessels being affected by wind or current. In this case, the course made good may differ substantially from the vessel's heading. It is clear from the Rule that the head-on situation is determined by the vessel's head, and not the course made good. Watch officers and vessel operators should make every attempt to be aware of prevailing current, so that they can make a better assessment of the situation. Course changes may have to be larger than normal to compensate for the leeway encountered.

current shall have the right-of-way over an upbound vessel, shall propose the manner of passage, and shall initiate the maneuvering signals prescribed by Rule 34(a)(*i*), as appropriate.

Rule 15. Crossing Situation

When two power-driven vessels are crossing so as to involve risk of collision, the vessel which has the other on her own starboard side shall keep out of the way and shall, if the circumstances of the case admit, avoid crossing ahead of the other vessel.

Rule 15. Crossing Situation

(a) When two power-driven vessels are crossing so as to involve risk of collision, the vessel which has the other on her starboard side shall keep out of the way and shall, if the circumstances of the case admit, avoid crossing ahead of the other vessel.

(b) Notwithstanding paragraph (a), on the Great Lakes, Western Rivers, or waters specified by the Secretary, a vessel crossing a river shall keep out of the way of a power-driven vessel ascending or descending the river.

When a vessel is in any doubt as to whether a head-on situation exists, she shall assume that it does. Therefore, she must take early and substantial action to keep well clear (Rule 16) and to ensure a port-to-port passing.

Rule 15.

A crossing situation is defined by the process of elimination. If a risk-of-collision situation does not meet the requirements of an overtaking situation (Rule 13) or a head-on situation (Rule 14), then it must be a crossing situation. When applying this Rule, it will help to keep in mind the situations which are affected by other Rules as well as this one. These situations include those:

1. In a narrow channel where one of the vessels can navigate only within the channel (Rule 9 (d));

2. In which one of the vessels is not under command, restricted in her ability to maneuver, engaged in fishing, or constrained by her draft (Rule 18);

3. In a traffic separation scheme (Rule 10) (i) and (j) involving small vessels, sailing vessels, or fishing vessels;

4. In which one or both of the vessels is a sailing vessel (Rule 12).

The Rule requires that a vessel in a crossing situation, with the other vessel to her starboard, shall keep out of the way. In so doing, she is cautioned to avoid crossing ahead of the other. This requirement fits nicely with the requirement in Rule 17; that a stand-on vessel taking action to avoid collision should avoid altering course to port. If both vessels take the appropriate action, then, a safer passing distance should be the result.

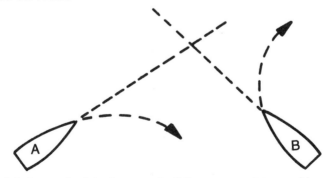

Vessel A is required to keep out of the way and to avoid crossing ahead. Vessel B is required to hold course and speed or, if taking action in accordance with Rule 17, avoid altering course to port.

Rule 16. Action by Give-way Vessel

Every vessel which is directed to keep out of the way of another vessel shall, so far as possible, take early and substantial action to keep well clear.

Rule 17. Action by Stand-on Vessel

(a) *(i)* Where one of two vessels is to keep out of the way the other shall keep her course and speed.

(ii) The latter vessel may however take action to avoid collision by her maneuver alone, as soon as it becomes apparent to her that the vessel required to keep out of the way is not taking appropriate action in compliance with these Rules.

A vessel that is stopped and making no way is not allowed to show any special signals or take any special privileges. Therefore, that vessel must be prepared to keep out of the way when involved in a crossing situation as the give-way vessel.

Rule 16.

Action taken in accordance with this Rule must also comply with the other applicable Rules. The action must fall within the guidelines of Rule 8, since Rule 8 applies in any condition of visibility. Consequently, the action taken must be positive, must be made in ample time, and must be checked for effectiveness until the other vessel is clear. Although Rule 16 states only that the vessel must keep clear, she must make certain not to violate any of the other Rules while doing so.

Rule 17.

The first thing to notice is that this Rule applies when "one of two vessels is to keep out of the way." Vessels which must "keep out of the way" of other vessels are mentioned in Rules 12, 13, 15, and 18. In order for a vessel to determine that she must take action to keep out of the way, she must determine if risk of collision exists. Therefore, for Rule 17 to apply, risk of collision must exist. As soon as the watch officer determines that his vessel is approaching another in a manner that involves risk of collision (see discussion on Rule 7), Rule 17 applies. The officer must then decide if he is operating the stand-on or the give-way vessel. If he is in charge of the stand-on vessel, the officer is bound by Rule 17 to hold course and speed. He must provide the give-way vessel

(b) When, from any cause, the vessel required to keep her course and speed finds herself so close that collision cannot be avoided by the action of the give-way vessel alone, she shall take such action as will best aid to avoid collision.

(c) A power-driven vessel which takes action in a crossing situation in accordance with sub-paragraph (a) *(ii)* of this Rule to avoid collision with another power-driven vessel shall, if the circumstances of the case admit, not alter course to port for a vessel on her own port side.

(d) This Rule does not relieve the give-way vessel of her obligation to keep out of the way.

an adequate opportunity to take appropriate action to keep out of the way. If the stand-on vessel takes action other than to hold course and speed, it will undoubtedly be held liable for any subsequent catastrophe resulting from that action. A stand-on vessel may take action to avoid collision *only* when "it becomes apparent to her that the vessel required to keep out of the way is not taking appropriate action in compliance with these Rules." To meet this condition, there must clearly be some observation of the give-way vessel for a time after the risk of collision was determined.

This Rule does not mention sounding the signal of doubt (danger signal) prescribed in Rule 34 (d). However, the stand-on vessel would usually be in doubt as to whether the give-way vessel was taking sufficient action before becoming certain that she was not. In this case, the vessel in doubt must sound at least five short and rapid blasts on the whistle (Rule 34 (d)). When sounded by a stand-on vessel in an approaching situation, this signal may alert the other vessel to the fact that reasonable doubt exists as to whether she is fulfilling her obligations according to the Rules. If the danger signal just described has the desired effect, further action by the stand-on vessel may be unnecessary.

When the stand-on vessel has determined that the give-way vessel is not taking appropriate action to avoid collision, she may herself maneuver to achieve that end. The only restriction placed on this action is that she should avoid altering course to port for a vessel on her own port side. One obvious reason for this requirement is the fact that, since the give-way vessel may still decide to take action, and since the Rules discourage the give-way vessel from crossing ahead of the other (Rule 15), she would likely change course to starboard. If the stand-on vessel was simultaneously changing course to port, the result could be most unfortunate.

This Rule does not force the stand-on vessel to take any action until she "finds herself so close that collision cannot be avoided by the action of the give-way vessel alone." This is the point known as "in extremis," and it should be pointed out that at this point collision can still be avoided, but not by the action of the give-way vessel alone. At the time of in extremis, and only then, is the stand-on vessel *required* by the Rules to take action. However, since the Rules allow her to take action prior to that stage commonly known as in extremis, she might well be found at least partially at fault for not doing so. If collision becomes imminent, the stand-on vessel should take such action as would best lessen the effects of the collision.

Rule 18. Responsibilities Between Vessels

Except where Rules 9, 10 and 13 otherwise require:

(a) A power-driven vessel underway shall keep out of the way of:

(i) a vessel not under command;

(ii) a vessel restricted in her ability to maneuver;

Let us, then, summarize the chronology of events that we have discussed. The watch officer on a vessel sights another vessel to port. He then:

1. *May* take action before risk of collision exists to avoid the situation,
2. Determines that risk of collision exists,
3. *Must* hold course and speed to provide opportunity for the give-way vessel to take action,
4. Becomes doubtful that the give-way vessel is taking appropriate action to avoid collision,
5. Sounds the danger signal,
6. Determines whether or not the danger signal provokes action from the give-way vessel,
7. Becomes convinced that the give-way vessel is not taking appropriate action,
8. May take action to avoid collision by his vessel's maneuver alone,
9. but if he does not take action earlier, he *must* take action when any maneuvers available to the give-way vessel will not, in themselves, prevent collision.

Paragraph (d) of this Rule reminds the give-way vessel that, regardless of actions taken by the stand-on vessel, nothing relieves the give-way vessel of her obligation to keep clear and, under normal circumstances, to bear most, if not all, the blame for any resulting mishap.

To conclude—when two vessels are crossing so as to involve risk of collision, there is only one point at which collision can occur if both vessels maintain course and speed. Therefore, if only one vessel alters course *or* speed, collision becomes a physical impossibility.* The object, then, is to avoid collision by as few maneuvers as possible, and preferably by only one of the vessels. Therefore, the stand-on vessel should not make any maneuvers until he is certain that the give-way vessel is not going to take appropriate action.

Rule 18.

The wording of this Rule is the same for inland and international waters. However, the Inland Rules do not address the subject of a vessel constrained by her draft, since under these Rules this designation does not exist.

The Rule begins with the phrase "except where Rules 9, 10, and 13 otherwise require." The Rule, then, does not cover all situations involving

---

*We should like to credit this synopsis to Commander E. J. Geissler, Nautical Science Dept., Maine Maritime Academy.

  (iii) a vessel engaged in fishing;

  (iv) a sailing vessel.

(b) A sailing vessel underway shall keep out of the way of:

  (i) a vessel not under command;

  (ii) a vessel restricted in her ability to maneuver;

  (iii) a vessel engaged in fishing.

(c) A vessel engaged in fishing when underway shall, so far as possible, keep out of the way of:

  (i) a vessel not under command;

  (ii) a vessel restricted in her ability to maneuver.

(d) *(i)* Any vessel other than a vessel not under command or a vessel restricted in her ability to maneuver shall, if the circumstances of the case admit, avoid impeding the safe passage of a vessel constrained by her draft, exhibiting the signals in Rule 28.

  (ii) A vessel constrained by her draft shall navigate with particular caution having full regard to her special condition.

(e) A seaplane on the water shall, in general, keep well clear of all vessels and avoid impeding their navigation. In circumstances, however, where risk of collision exists, she shall comply with the Rules of this Part.

(d) A seaplane on the water shall, in general, keep well clear of all vessels and avoid impeding their navigation. In circumstances, however, where risk of collision exists, she shall comply with the Rules of this Part.

the vessels mentioned. Rule 9 applies to vessels in narrow channels, Rule 10, to traffic separation schemes, and Rule 13, to overtaking situations. These Rules supersede Rule 18. After insuring that one of the exceptions is not the Rule, we may proceed to discuss the Rule itself. The definitions for the terms used in this Rule are found in Rule 3.

In order to claim a privilege by virtue of Rule 18, a vessel must be showing appropriate lights and/or shapes so that other vessels can readily recognize her condition, and she must meet the requirements of the applicable definition. A power-driven vessel is obliged to keep out of the way of the other vessels listed in the Rule. She must do this any time she is underway. If she is underway, but stopped, and not making way, she is still under obligation to fulfill this responsibility.

Because of the operational restrictions present in any situation involving any of the vessels mentioned by this Rule, the give-way vessel cannot reasonably expect that the stand-on vessel will be able to hold its course and speed as required by Rule 17 (a) *(ii)*, unless the hampered vessel is dead in the water. The give-way vessel should give as wide a berth as possible in these situations, realizing that the stand-on vessel may not have much control over its own movements, and that the entire burden of avoiding collision may well fall to the give-way vessel. Since special lights and shapes are sometimes difficult to distinguish, the stand-on vessel in these situations should be aware that the other vessel may not recognize the situation, and should be ready to sound the danger signal (Rule 34 (d)) if the give-way vessel does not seem to be taking appropriate action. Also, a vessel which in most circumstances would consider herself the stand-on vessel (such as a fishing vessel) should not take her privilege for granted, but should keep a sharp lookout lest the other vessel involved be even more privileged (such as a vessel restricted in her ability to maneuver). The Rule establishes a type of pecking order which, it is hoped, will aid in the determination of responsibilities between the vessels.

This Rule also requires a power-driven vessel to keep out of the way of a sailing vessel. However, as discussed previously (Rule 9), the sailing vessel is usually smaller, more maneuverable, and has greater opportunity to avoid collision by taking action to avoid the situation entirely, or by applying Rule 17 (a) *(ii)* and taking action by her maneuver alone.

Paragraphs (a) and (b) of the Rule use the term "shall keep out of the way." Paragraph (c) states that a fishing vessel "shall, so far as possible, keep out of the way." The Rule recognizes that a vessel engaged in fishing may find it almost impossible to keep out of the way of another

vessel. This depends, usually, on the type of gear employed by the fishing vessel. Other vessels may have similar difficulties in fulfilling their responsibilities; hence the wording "if the circumstances of the case admit" in paragraph (d) *(i)*. Also, there may be cases where such situations could be classified as "special circumstances" under Rule 2 (b), thus requiring the vessels to depart from the Rules to avoid immediate danger.

It should be remembered that because a vessel falls into one of the categories in this Rule, it is not necessarily travelling at a slow rate of speed. Trawlers are not required by the Rules to stand still, and vessels that are not under command may have the throttle stuck open. A vessel that is constrained by her draft may well be operating at full speed within the channel. She is, however, instructed by the Rule to "navigate with particular caution." It is doubtful that any watch officer would ever admit to navigating with "less than particular caution," and unfortunately collisions occur with remarkable regularity between vessels being so navigated. Therefore, perhaps the best advice is simply to strive to navigate with a little "more particular caution," especially when encountering any of the situations outlined in this Rule.

I I I

CONDUCT OF VESSELS IN RESTRICTED VISIBILITY

Rule 19. Conduct of Vessels in Restricted Visibility

(a) This Rule applies to vessels not in sight of one another when navigating in or near an area of restricted visibility.

(b) Every vessel shall proceed at a safe speed adapted to the prevailing circumstances and conditions of restricted visibility. A power-driven vessel shall have her engines ready for immediate maneuver.

(c) Every vessel shall have due regard to the prevailing circumstances and conditions of restricted visibility when complying with the Rules of Section I of this Part.

(d) A vessel which detects by radar alone the presence of another vessel shall determine if a close-quarters situation is developing and/or risk of collision exists. If so, she shall take avoiding action in ample time, provided that when such action consists of an alteration of course, so far as possible the following shall be avoided:

(c) Every vessel shall have due regard to the prevailing circumstances and conditions of restricted visibility when complying with Rules 4 through 10.

(d) A vessel which detects by radar alone the presence of another vessel shall determine if a close-quarters situation is developing or risk of collision exists. If so, she shall take avoiding action in ample time, provided that when such action consists of an alteration of course, so far as possible the following shall be avoided:

Rule 19.

Rule 19 is an excellent example of the necessity of keeping a proper and vigilant lookout. The Rule applies only to vessels "*not* in sight of one another." We may tend to think this Rule applies at any time visibility is restricted, but such is not the case. If, when operating in restricted visibility, the other vessel can be seen visually, this Rule does not apply. Therefore, it is vital that we employ the Rule *only* when we cannot visually observe the other vessel.

Rule 19 also applies to vessels "navigating in or *near* an area of restricted visibility." This means that if you are in an area of good visibility but can see a fog bank, rainstorm, or other area of restricted visibility, you are responsible to abide by the provisions of this Rule. Remember, there may be a vessel in the fog bank not aware of your presence.

In addition, the Rule addresses the subject of safe speed, which is to be "adapted to the prevailing circumstances and conditions of restricted visibility." The unavoidable inference here is that this "safe speed" may well be a different speed than the "safe speed" mentioned in Rule 6. The first factor to be taken into account when determining safe speed (in Rule 6) is "the state of visibility." The idea contained here seems to be that the

(i) an alteration of course to port for a vessel forward of the beam, other than for a vessel being overtaken;

(i) an alteration of course to port for a vessel forward of the beam, other than for a vessel being overtaken; and

(ii) an alteration of course toward a vessel abeam or abaft the beam.

(e) Except where it has been determined that a risk of collision does not exist, every vessel which hears apparently forward of her beam the fog signal of another vessel, or which cannot avoid a close-quarters situation with another vessel forward of her beam, shall reduce her speed to the minimum at which she can be kept on her course. She shall if necessary take all her way off and in any event navigate with extreme caution until danger of collision is over.

more restricted the visibility becomes, the more restricted a safe speed becomes. Since to apply Rule 19 we have already admitted that the visibility is restricted to such a degree that we cannot see other vessels, we must admit that when we adapt the safe speed of Rule 6 to the visibility conditions required by Rule 19, the result is a reduced speed requirement. In almost every case of a collision in fog, one or both of the vessels is cited for proceeding at an excessive rate of speed for the existing visibility conditions. The speed requirement is coupled with the requirement that "a power-driven vessel shall have her engines ready for immediate maneuver."

Paragraph (c) is a reminder that, since the Rules (4 through 10) in Section I apply in any condition of visibility, Rule 19 applies *in addition to* (and not separate from) those Rules when visibility is restricted.

Paragraph (d) addresses the problem of a situation involving risk of collision in restricted visibility. Such a situation can be detected only by radar. If you can determine by radar that a close-quarters situation is developing, you are required to "take avoiding action in ample time." It does not matter where the other vessel is located, or whether your vessel would ordinarily have the right of way. There is no right of way, no stand-on vessel, no give-way vessel, and no time for playing waiting games.

This Rule takes the negative approach and tells you what you should avoid doing. The options available to you are the following:

1. If the vessel is anywhere forward of either beam, you may
   (a) adjust your speed
   (b) alter course to starboard
   (c) do both of the above in any proportion you see fit

The Rule states that the exception to this course of action is an instance when you are overtaking another vessel. To overtake another vessel in visibility restricted to the extent that you cannot see her is an extremely hazardous maneuver and should be avoided. When it is determined that such a situation exists, the overtaking vessel should take early action to give the other vessel plenty of sea room.

2. If the vessel is abaft your beam, you may
   (a) adjust your speed
   (b) alter course away from the vessel
   (c) do both of the above in any proportion you see fit.

The actions recommended by this Rule will result in the same passing processes as the actions required by vessels in sight of one another. They are simply being stated in a different way.

Remember that while operating in visibility conditions that require the application of Rule 19, the vessels involved will be sounding fog signals. If, however, the vessels come in sight of one another, Rule 19 no longer applies, and the vessels must then apply the Rules for vessels in sight.

Paragraph (e) requires that, unless you have determined that there is no risk of collision, anytime you hear a fog signal that is apparently coming from a direction forward of the beam, you are to slow to bare steerageway and take all way off your vessel, if necessary. It is sometimes a temptation to alter course away from a fog signal. This temptation should be avoided at all costs. Fog signals should not be used to determine a vessel's position. A fog signal's direction may be especially deceptive if the hearer is high on the vessel.

PART C
LIGHTS AND SHAPES

Rule 20. Application

(a) Rules in this Part shall be complied with in all weathers.

(b) The Rules concerning lights shall be complied with from sunset to sunrise, and during such times no other lights shall be exhibited, except such lights as cannot be mistaken for the lights specified in these Rules or do not impair their visibility or distinctive character, or interfere with the keeping of a proper look-out.

(c) The lights prescribed by these Rules shall, if carried, also be exhibited from sunrise to sunset in restricted visibility and may be exhibited in all other circumstances when it is deemed necessary.

(d) The Rules concerning shapes shall be complied with by day.

(e) The lights and shapes specified in these Rules shall comply with the provisions of Annex I to these Regulations.

(e) The lights and shapes specified in these Rules shall comply with the provisions of Annex I of these Rules.

Rule 21. Definitions

(a) "Masthead light" means a white light placed over the fore and aft centerline of the vessel showing an unbroken light over an arc of the horizon of 225 degrees and so fixed as to

Rule 21. Definitions

(a) "Masthead light" means a white light placed over the fore and aft centerline of the vessel showing an unbroken light over an arc of the horizon of 225 degrees and so fixed as to

Rule 20.

This Rule seems fairly clear. Basically, it states that the lights which will be discussed in the following Rules must be exhibited at night or any time when the visibility is restricted. Many vessels leave their lights on whenever they are underway—a practice that is hard to fault as long as the lights are appropriate.

Paragraph (e) refers the reader to Annex I of the Rules, which includes the specifications for the required lights.

For convenience the many Rules with lighting requirements for vessels have been arranged in the form of a table. It may seem complicated at first but it should prove easy to use as you become familiar with it. Most of the references in the body of the table are either back to lines A or B (which are lights for power-driven vessels), or are back to the previous column in the same line.

For instance, if you want to find the lights shown by a power-driven vessel towing astern on inland waters, not making way, you would go to line (G), column (3). The table informs you that these lights are the same as the previous column (G2). You now know that this vessel shows the same lights whether making way or not. (G2) refers you to (A2) or (B2), which are the lights for power-driven vessels, and then gives the additional requirements for a vessel towing. The key to understanding the table is a familiarity with the lines (A) and (B). Since every student of the Rules needs to know these requirements anyway, the following table should not be difficult to master.

	1 Vessel	2 Underway and Making Way	3 Underway and Stopped	4 At Anchor
A	power-driven vessel 50 meters or longer (Int. and Inl.)	• forward masthead light • after masthead light • sidelights • sternlight	same as (A2)	• forward all-round light, or ball • after all-round light • may use working lights under 100 meters • must use working lights 100 meters and up
	Vessel aground shows anchor lights plus two red lights or three balls in a vertical line.			
B	power-driven vessel less than 50 meters (Int. and Inl.)	same as (A2) • after masthead light optional	same as (B2)	same as (A4) or, all-round light where best seen
	Vessel aground shows anchor lights plus two red lights or three balls in a vertical line.			
C	air cushion vessel in non-displacement mode (Int. and Inl.)	same as (A2) except an additional all-round flashing yellow light	same as (C2)	NA (Not Applicable)
D	power-driven vessel length under 12 meters (Int. and Inl.)	same as (B2), or • one all-round white light • sidelights (Inl.) • sidelights, if practicable (Int.)	same as (D2)	same as (B4)

	1 Vessel	2 Underway and Making Way	3 Underway and Stopped	4 At Anchor
E	power-driven vessel (Great Lakes only)	same as (A2), except • may show all-round white light in lieu of after masthead light and sternlight	same as (E2)	same as (A4)
F	power-driven vessel towing astern (Int.)	same as (A2) or (B2) except • two forward or after masthead lights in a vertical line (three if tow over 200 meters) • towing light above sternlight • diamond shape (tow over 200 meters)	same as (F2)	NA
G	power-driven vessel towing astern (Inl.)	same as (A2) or (B2) except • two masthead lights instead of either the forward or after masthead light (three if tow over 200 meters) • towing light above the sternlight • diamond shape (tow over 200 meters)	same as (G2)	NA
H	power-driven vessel pushing ahead or alongside (Int.)	same as (A2) or (B2) except • two forward or after masthead lights in a vertical line	same as (H2)	NA

	1 Vessel	2 Underway and Making Way	3 Underway and Stopped	4 At Anchor
I	power-driven vessel pushing ahead or alongside (Inl.)	same as (A2) or (B2) except • two masthead lights instead of either the forward or after masthead light • two towing lights in a vertical line instead of the sternlight	same as (I2)	same as (A4) or (B4), depending on length

A vessel pushing ahead or alongside on Western Rivers waters will carry the towing lights, but no masthead lights. (Rule 24(i))

	1 Vessel	2 Underway and Making Way	3 Underway and Stopped	4 At Anchor
J	vessel being towed (Int. and Inl.)	• sidelights • sternlight • diamond shape (tow over 200 meters)	same as (J2)	same as (A4) or (B4), depending on length

Any number of vessels towed alongside or pushed in group shall be lighted as one vessel. See additional requirements for vessels towed. (Rule 24 (e), (f), (g), (h))

	1 Vessel	2 Underway and Making Way	3 Underway and Stopped	4 At Anchor
K	sailing vessel (Int. and Inl.)	• sidelights • sternlight • red over green all-round lights on the mast (optional)	same as (K2)	same as (A4) or (B4), depending on length

On sailing vessels less than 20 meters, running lights may be in combined lantern on mast.
If lights are in combined lantern, red over green lights may not be carried.
Any sail vessel (Int.) and one 12 meters or over (Inl.), also propelled by machinery, shall exhibit a conical shape, apex downward.

	1 Vessel	2 Underway and Making Way	3 Underway and Stopped	4 At Anchor
L	vessel engaged in trawling (Int. and Inl.)	• green over white all-round lights in a vertical line • masthead light abaft and higher than the green light (optional under 50 meters) • sidelights • sternlight	same as (L2) except sidelights and sternlight extinguished	same as (L3)
	Day shape consists of two cones, apexes together, in a vertical line. A vessel less than 20 meters may show a basket.			
M	vessel engaged in fishing other than trawling (Int. and Inl.)	• red over white all-round lights in a vertical line • if gear extends more than 150 meters, an all-round white light or cone, apex upwards, in direction of gear. • sidelights • sternlight • same day shape as trawler	same as (M2) except sidelights and sternlight extinguished	same as (M3)
	Vessels fishing in close proximity may show additional signals—Annex II of Rules.			
N	vessel not under command (Int. and Inl.)	• two all-round red lights in a vertical line or two balls • sidelights • sternlight	same as (N2) except sidelights and sternlight extinguished	NA by definition, a vessel not under command is underway see Rule 3 (f)

1 Vessel	2 Underway and Making Way	3 Underway and Stopped	4 At Anchor
O	vessel restricted in her ability to maneuver (except mineclearance) (Int. and Inl.)	• red over white over red all-round lights • masthead lights • sidelights • sternlight • ball over diamond over ball	same as (O2) except masthead lights, sidelights, and sternlight extinguished	(A4) or (B4) plus (O3)
P	vessel engaged in mineclearance (Int. and Inl.)	• masthead lights • sidelights • sternlight • three green lights or three balls one at foremasthead and one at each end of foreyard	same as (P2)	NA vessel must be underway
Q	vessel towing, unable to deviate from her course (Int. and Inl.)	• (F2) or (G2) plus • red over white over red all-round lights • ball over diamond over ball	same as Q2	NA
R	vessel engaged in dredging or underwater operations (Int. and Inl.)	same as (O2) and, when obstruction exists, • two red lights or two balls in a vertical line on side of obstruction • two green lights or two diamonds in a vertical line on clear side	same as (R2) except masthead lights, sidelights, and sternlight extinguished	same as (R3)

	1 Vessel	2 Underway and Making Way	3 Underway and Stopped	4 At Anchor
S	vessel constrained by her draft	(A2) plus • three red lights in a vertical line • a cylinder	same as (S2)	same as (A4)
T	pilot vessel	• white over red all-round lights • sidelights • sternlight	same as (T2)	(A4) or (B4) plus • white over red all-round lights

show the light from right ahead to 22.5 degrees abaft the beam on either side of the vessel.

(b) "Sidelights" means a green light on the starboard side and a red light on the port side each showing an unbroken light over an arc of the horizon of 112.5 degrees and so fixed as to show the light from right ahead to 22.5 degrees abaft the beam on its respective side. In a vessel of less than 20 meters in length the sidelights may be combined in one lantern carried on the fore and aft centerline of the vessel.

show the light from right ahead to 22.5 degrees abaft the beam on either side of the vessel, except that on a vessel of less than 12 meters in length the masthead light shall be placed as nearly as practicable to the fore and aft centerline of the vessel.

(b) "Sidelights" means a green light on the starboard side and a red light on the port side each showing an unbroken light over an arc of the horizon of 112.5 degrees and so fixed as to show the light from right ahead to 22.5 degrees abaft the beam on its respective side. On a vessel of less than 20 meters in length the sidelights may be combined in one lantern carried on the fore and aft centerline of the vessel, except that on a vessel of less than 12 meters in length the sidelights when combined in one lantern shall be placed as nearly as practicable to the fore and aft centerline of the vessel.

(c) "Sternlight" means a white light placed as nearly as practicable at the stern showing an unbroken light over an arc of the horizon of 135 degrees and so fixed as to show the light 67.5 degrees from right aft on each side of the vessel.

(d) "Towing light" means a yellow light having the same characteristics as the "sternlight" defined in paragraph (c) of this Rule.

Masthead Light

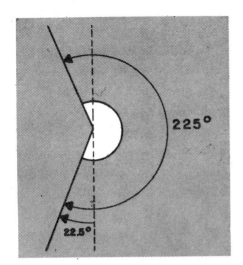

The masthead light shall be on the centerline, except that on a vessel less than 12 meters in length in Inland waters, the masthead light shall be placed as nearly as practicable to the centerline.

Sidelights

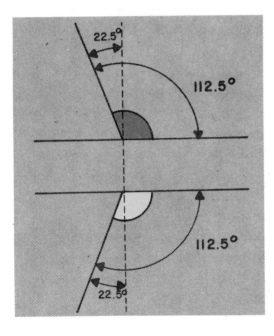

In vessels of less than 20 meters in length the sidelights may be combined in one lantern on the fore and aft centerline, except that on a vessel less than 12 meters in length in Inland waters, the sidelights when combined in one lantern shall be placed as nearly as practicable to the fore and aft centerline of the vessel.

(e) "All-round light" means a light showing an unbroken light over an arc of the horizon of 360 degrees.

(f) "Flashing light" means a light flashing at regular intervals at a frequency of 120 flashes or more per minute.

(g) "Special flashing light" means a yellow light flashing at regular intervals at a frequency of 50 to 70 flashes per minute, placed as far forward and as nearly as practicable on the fore and aft centerline of the tow and showing an unbroken light over an arc of the horizon of not less than 180 degress nor more than 225 degress and so fixed as to show the light from right ahead to abeam and no more than 22.5 degrees abaft the beam on either side of the vessel.

Rule 22. Visibility of Lights

The lights prescribed in these Rules shall have an intensity as specified in Section 8 of Annex I to these Regulations so as to be visible at the following minimum ranges:

(a) In vessels of 50 meters or more in length:
  a masthead light, 6 miles;
  a sidelight, 3 miles;
  a sternlight, 3 miles;
  a towing light, 3 miles;
  a white, red, green or yellow
   all-round light, 3 miles.

Rule 22. Visibility of Lights

The lights prescribed in these Rules shall have an intensity as specified in Annex I to these Rules, so as to be visible at the following minimum ranges:

(a) In a vessel of 50 meters or more in length:
  a masthead light, 6 miles;
  a sidelight, 3 miles;
  a sternlight, 3 miles;
  a towing light, 3 miles;
  a white, red, green or yellow
   all-round light, 3 miles;
   and
  a special flashing light,
   2 miles.

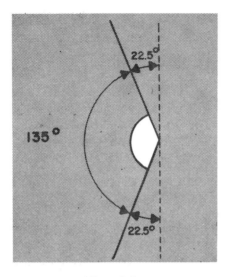

Stern light

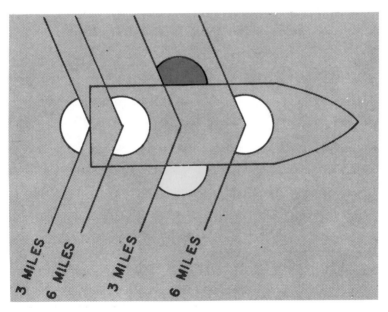

Vessel over 50 meters

(b) In vessels of 12 meters or more in length but less than 50 meters in length:
    a masthead light, 5 miles; except that where the length of the vessel is less than 20 meters, 3 miles;
    a sidelight, 2 miles;
    a sternlight, 2 miles;
    a towing light, 2 miles;
    a white, red, green or yellow all-round light, 2 miles.

(c) In vessels of less than 12 meters in length:
    a masthead light, 2 miles;
    a sidelight, 1 mile;
    a sternlight, 2 miles;
    a towing light, 2 miles;
    a white, red, green or yellow all-round light, 2 miles.

(d) In inconspicuous, partly submerged vessels or objects being towed:
    a white all-round light, 3 miles.

Rule 23. Power-driven Vessels Underway

(a) A power-driven vessel underway shall exhibit:
    (i) a masthead light forward;

(b) In a vessel of 12 meters or more in length but less than 50 meters in length:
    a masthead light, 5 miles; except that where the length of the vessel is less than 20 meters, 3 miles;
    a sidelight, 2 miles;
    a sternlight, 2 miles;
    a towing light, 2 miles;
    a white, red, green or yellow all-round light, 2 miles; and a special flashing light, 2 miles.

(c) In a vessel of less than 12 meters in length:
    a masthead light, 2 miles;
    a sidelight, 1 mile;
    a sternlight, 2 miles;
    a towing light, 2 miles;
    a white, red, green or yellow all-round light, 2 miles; and a special flashing light, 2 miles.

(d) In an inconspicuous, partly submerged vessel or object being towed:
    a white all-round light, 3 miles.

Rule 23. Power-driven Vessels Underway

(a) A power-driven vessel underway shall exhibit:
    (i) a masthead light forward; except that a vessel of less than 20 meters in length

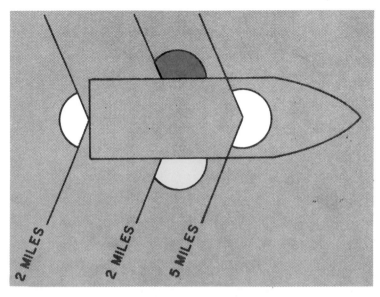

Vessel between 12 and 50 meters

The masthead light on vessels less than 20 meters in length must be visible for at least 3 miles instead of 5 miles. On a vessel of less than 20 meters in length, the sidelights may be combined in one lantern.

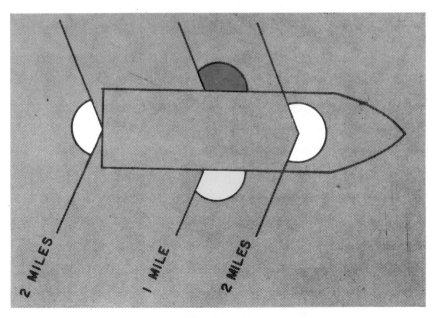

Vessel less than 12 meters

On a vessel of less than 20 meters in length, the sidelights may be combined in one lantern.

(ii) a second masthead light abaft of and higher than the forward one; except that a vessel of less than 50 meters in length shall not be obliged to exhibit such light but may do so;

(iii) sidelights;

(iv) a sternlight.

(b) An air-cushion vessel when operating in the non-displacement mode shall, in addition to the lights prescribed in paragraph (a) of this Rule, exhibit an all-round flashing yellow light.

(c) *(i)* A power-driven vessel of less than 12 meters in length may in lieu of the lights prescribed in paragraph (a) of this Rule exhibit an all-round white light and sidelights;

(ii) a power-driven vessel of less than 7 meters in length whose maximum speed does not exceed 7 knots may in lieu of the lights prescribed in paragraph (a) of this Rule exhibit an all-round white light and shall, if practicable, also exhibit sidelights;

(iii) the masthead light or all-round white light on a power-driven vessel of less than 12 meters in length may

need not exhibit this light forward of amidships but shall exhibit it as far forward as is practicable;

(ii) a second masthead light abaft of and higher than the forward one; except that a vessel of less than 50 meters in length shall not be obliged to exhibit such light but may do so;

(iii) sidelights; and

(iv) a sternlight.

(b) An air-cushion vessel when operating in the nondisplacement mode shall, in addition to the lights prescribed in paragraph (a) of this Rule, exhibit an all-round flashing yellow light where it can best be seen.

(c) A power-driven vessel of less than 12 meters in length may, in lieu of the lights prescribed in paragraph (a) of this Rule, exhibit an all-round white light and sidelights.

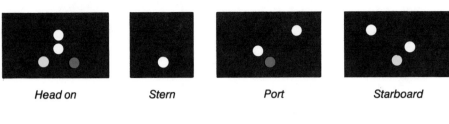

| Head on | Stern | Port | Starboard |

Power-driven vessel 50 meters or longer

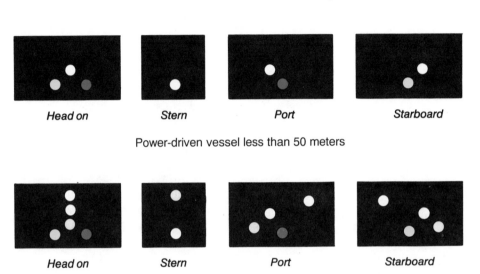

| Head on | Stern | Port | Starboard |

Power-driven vessel less than 50 meters

| Head on | Stern | Port | Starboard |

Air-cushion vessel in non-displacement mode—yellow light is flashing

All views

Power-driven vessel less than 7 meters (international waters)

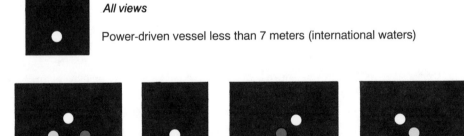

| Head on | Stern | Port | Starboard |

Power-driven vessel less than 12 meters—sidelights may be combined

be displaced from the fore and aft centerline of the vessel if centerline fitting is not practicable, provided that the sidelights are combined in one lantern which shall be carried on the fore and aft centerline of the vessel or located as nearly as practicable in the same fore and aft line as the masthead light or the all-round white light.

(d) A power-driven vessel when operating on the Great Lakes may carry an all-round white light in lieu of the second masthead light and sternlight prescribed in paragraph (a) of this Rule. The light shall be carried in the position of the second masthead light and be visible at the same minimum range.

Rule 24. Towing and Pushing

(a) A power-driven vessel when towing shall exhibit:

(*i*) instead of the light prescribed in Rule 23 (a) (*i*) or (a) (*ii*), two masthead lights in a vertical line. When the length of the tow, measuring from the stern of the towing vessel to the after end of the tow exceeds 200 meters, three such lights in a vertical line;

(*ii*) sidelights;

(*iii*) a sternlight;

Rule 24. Towing and Pushing

(a) A power-driven vessel when towing astern shall exhibit:

(*i*) instead of the light prescribed either in Rule 23 (a) (*i*) or 23 (a) (*ii*), two masthead lights in a vertical line. When the length of the tow, measuring from the stern of the towing vessel to the after end of the tow exceeds 200 meters, three such lights in a vertical line;

(*ii*) sidelights;

(*iii*) a sternlight;

Head on   *Stern*   *Port*

Vessel less than 50 meters with tow 200 meters or less in length

 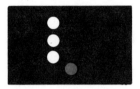

Head on   *Stern*   *Port*   *Day shape*

Vessel less than 50 meters with tow over 200 meters

Head on   *Stern*   *Port*

Vessel 50 meters or more with tow 200 meters or less
Vessel may carry the two lights in place of the after masthead light
(one light forward and two aft)

Head on   *Stern*   *Port*   *Day shape*

Vessel 50 meters or more with tow over 200 meters
Vessel may carry the three lights in place of the after masthead light
(one light forward and three aft)

(iv) a towing light in a vertical line above the sternlight;

(iv) a towing light in a vertical line above the sternlight; and

(v) when the length of the tow exceeds 200 meters, a diamond shape where it can best be seen.

(b) When a pushing vessel and a vessel being pushed ahead are rigidly connected in a composite unit they shall be regarded as a power-driven vessel and exhibit the lights prescribed in Rule 23.

(c) A power-driven vessel when pushing ahead or towing alongside, except in the case of a composite unit, shall exhibit:

(c) A power-driven vessel when pushing ahead or towing alongside, except as required by paragraphs (b) and (i) of this Rule, shall exhibit:

(i) instead of the light prescribed in Rule 23 (a) *(i)* or (a) *(ii)*, two masthead lights in a vertical line;

(i) instead of the light prescribed either in Rule 23 (a) *(i)* or 23 (a) *(ii)*, two masthead lights in a vertical line;

(ii) sidelights;

(iii) a sternlight.

(ii) sidelights; and

(iii) two towing lights in a vertical line.

(d) A power-driven vessel to which paragraph (a) or (c) of this Rule apply shall also comply with Rule 23 (a) *(ii)*.

(d) A power-driven vessel to which paragraphs (a) or (c) of this Rule apply shall also comply with Rule 23 (a) *(i)* and 23 (a) *(ii)*.

(e) A vessel or object being towed, other than those mentioned in paragraph (g) of this Rule, shall exhibit:

(e) A vessel or object other than those referred to in paragraph (g) of this Rule being towed shall exhibit:

(i) sidelights;

(ii) a sternlight;

(iii) when the length of the tow exceeds 200 meters, a diamond shape where it can best be seen.

(i) sidelights;

(ii) a sternlight; and

(iii) when the length of the tow exceeds 200 meters, a diamond shape where it can best be seen.

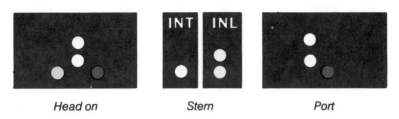

Head on   Stern   Port

Vessel less than 50 meters pushing ahead or towing alongside

Head on   Stern   Port

Vessel 50 meters or more pushing ahead or towing alongside
Vessel may carry the two lights in place of the after masthead light
(one light forward and two aft)

Rule 24 (d) (Inland)—At first reading, it might appear that we are now being required to display additional masthead lights, after we just replaced them with the vertical identifying lights required by paragraphs (a) and (c). Such is not the case. This paragraph is merely telling us, in a confusing way, that if we carry our identifying lights in the position described in 23 (a) *(i)*[forward], we must still comply with Rule 23 (a) *(ii)*; that is, carry an after masthead light if our vessel is over 50 meters in length. If we carry our identifying lights in the position described in 23 (a) *(ii)* [aft], we must still comply with Rule 23 (a) *(i)*; that is, carry a forward masthead light.

The Rules do not seem to mention more than one vessel towed astern, but such tows, such as a group of barges lashed together and towed on a bridle, should also be lighted as one vessel, lest a very confusing array be the result.

(f) Provided that any number of vessels being towed alongside or pushed in a group shall be lighted as one vessel,

    (i) a vessel being pushed ahead, not being part of a composite unit, shall exhibit at the forward end, sidelights;

    (ii) a vessel being towed alongside shall exhibit a sternlight and at the forward end, sidelights.

(g) An inconspicuous, partly submerged vessel or object, or combination of such vessels or objects being towed, shall exhibit:

    (i) if it is less than 25 meters in breadth, one all round white light at or near the forward end and one at or near the after end except that dracones need not exhibit a light at or near the forward end;

    (ii) if it is 25 meters or more in breadth, two additional all-round white lights at or near the extremities of its breadth;

    (iii) if it exceeds 100 meters in length, additional all-round white lights between the lights prescribed in sub-paragraphs *(i)* and *(ii)* so that the distance between the lights shall not exceed 100 meters;

(f) Provided that any number of vessels being towed alongside or pushed in a group shall be lighted as one vessel:

    (i) a vessel being pushed ahead, not being part of a composite unit, shall exhibit at the forward end sidelights, and a special flashing light; and

    (ii) a vessel being towed alongside shall exhibit a sternlight and at the forward end sidelights.

(g) An inconspicuous, partly submerged vessel or object being towed shall exhibit:

    (i) if it is less than 25 meters in breadth, one all-round white light at or near each end;

    (ii) if it is 25 meters or more in breadth, four all-round white lights to mark its length and breadth;

    (iii) if it exceeds 100 meters in length, additional all-round white lights between the lights prescribed in sub-paragraphs *(i)* and *(ii)* so that the distance between lights shall not exceed 100 meters; *Provided,* That any vessels or objects being towed alongside each other shall be lighted as one vessel or object;

Rule 24 (International)—A question has arisen as to whether a vessel engaged in towing, and exhibiting her identification lights in the after position, is required to carry a forward light. This question may be answered by noting that the Rule provides for substitution of the identifying lights for the existing lights, as follows:

1. The rule states that a vessel can exhibit two or three lights in a vertical line "instead of the light prescribed in 23 (a) *(i)* or 23 (a) *(ii)*."

2. The light prescribed in 23 (a) *(ii)* is, by definition, a "second light, abaft of and higher than the forward one."

3. Conclusion: By direct substitution, the identification lights, when substituted for those in 23 (a) *(ii)* [aft], must be "second light(s), abaft of and higher than the forward one." Therefore, there *must* be a forward light. The only exception to this requirement is allowed by Annex I (3) (b) for vessels less than 20 meters in length.

(iv) a diamond shape at or near the aftermost extremity of the last vessel or object being towed and if the length of the tow exceeds 200 meters an additional diamond shape where it can best be seen and located as far forward as is practicable.

(h) Where from any sufficient cause it is impracticable for a vessel or object being towed to exhibit the lights or shapes prescribed in paragraph (e) or (g) of this Rule, all possible measures shall be taken to light the vessel or object towed or at least to indicate the presence of such vessel or object.

(i) Where from any sufficient cause it is impracticable for a vessel not normally engaged in towing operations to display the lights prescribed in paragraph (a) or (c) of this Rule, such vessel shall not be required to exhibit those lights when engaged in towing another vessel in distress or otherwise in need of assistance. All possible measures shall be taken to indicate the nature of the relationship between the towing vessel and the vessel being towed as authorized by Rule 36, in particular by illuminating the towline.

(iv) a diamond shape at or near the aftermost extremity of the last vessel or object being towed; and

(v) the towing vessel may direct a searchlight in the direction of the tow to indicate its presence to an approaching vessel.

(h) Where from any sufficient cause it is impracticable for a vessel or object being towed to exhibit the lights prescribed in paragraph (e) or (g) of this Rule, all possible measures shall be taken to light the vessel or object towed or at least to indicate the presence of the unlighted vessel or object.

(i) Notwithstanding paragraph (c), on the Western Rivers (except below the Huey P. Long Bridge on the Mississippi River) and on waters specified by the Secretary, a power-driven vessel when pushing ahead or towing alongside, except as paragraph (b) applies, shall exhibit:

(i) sidelights; and

(ii) two towing lights in a vertical line.

(j) Where from any sufficient cause it is impracticable for a vessel not normally engaged in towing operations to

display the lights prescribed by paragraph (a), (c) or (i) of this Rule, such vessel shall not be required to exhibit those lights when engaged in towing another vessel in distress or otherwise in need of assistance. All possible measures shall be taken to indicate the nature of the relationship between the towing vessel and the vessel being assisted. The searchlight authorized by Rule 36 may be used to illuminate the tow.

Rule 25. Sailing Vessels Underway and Vessels Under Oars

(a) A sailing vessel underway shall exhibit:

　　(i) sidelights;

　　(ii) a sternlight.

(b) In a sailing vessel of less than 20 meters in length the lights prescribed in paragraph (a) of this Rule may be combined in one lantern carried at or near the top of the mast where it can best be seen.

(c) A sailing vessel underway may, in addition to the lights prescribed in paragraph (a) of this Rule, exhibit at or near the top of the mast, where they can best be seen, two all-round lights in a vertical line, the upper being red and the lower green, but these lights shall not be exhibited in conjunction with the combined lantern permitted by paragraph (b) of this Rule.

(d) *(i)* A sailing vessel of less than 7 meters in length shall, if practicable, exhibit the lights prescribed in paragraph

(a) or (b) of this Rule, but if she does not, she shall have ready at hand an electric torch or lighted lantern showing a white light which shall be exhibited in sufficient time to prevent collision.

(ii) A vessel under oars may exhibit the lights prescribed in this Rule for sailing vessels, but if she does not, she shall have ready at hand an electric torch or lighted lantern showing a white light which shall be exhibited in sufficient time to prevent a collision.

(e) A vessel proceeding under sail when also being propelled by machinery shall exhibit forward where it can best be seen a conical shape, apex downward.

(e) A vessel proceeding under sail when also being propelled by machinery shall exhibit forward where it can best be seen a conical shape, apex downward. A vessel of less than 12 meters in length is not required to exhibit this shape, but may do so.

Rule 26. Fishing Vessels

(a) A vessel engaged in fishing, whether underway or at anchor, shall exhibit only the lights and shapes prescribed in this Rule.

(b) A vessel when engaged in trawling, by which is meant the dragging through the water of a dredge net or other apparatus used as a fishing appliance, shall exhibit:

(i) two all-round lights in a vertical line, the upper being green and the lower white, or a shape consisting of two cones with their apexes together in a vertical line one above the other; a vessel of less than 20 meters in length may instead of this shape exhibit a basket;

Head on

Stern

Port

Sailing vessel with optional mast lights

Head on

Stern

Port

Day shape
Under sail be-
ing propelled
by machinery

Sailing vessel less than 20 meters (International and Inland)

Head on

Stern

Port

Day Shape
Basket if under
20 meters

Vessel less than 50 meters—trawling—underway—making way

Head on

Stern

Port

Day shape

Vessel 50 meters or more—trawling—underway—making way

(ii) a masthead light abaft of and higher than the all-round green light; a vessel of less than 50 meters in length shall not be obliged to exhibit such a light but may do so;

(iii) when making way through the water, in addition to the lights prescribed in this paragraph, sidelights and a sternlight.

(c) A vessel engaged in fishing, other than trawling, shall exhibit:

(i) two all-round lights in a vertical line, the upper being red and the lower white, or a shape consisting of two cones with apexes together in a vertical line one above the other; a vessel of less than 20 meters in length may instead of this shape exhibit a basket;

(ii) when there is outlying gear extending more than 150 meters horizontally from the vessel, an all-round white light or a cone apex upwards in the direction of the gear;

(iii) when making way through the water, in addition to the lights prescribed in this paragraph, sidelights and a sternlight.

(d) A vessel engaged in fishing in close proximity to other vessels engaged in fishing may exhibit the additional signals described in Annex II to these Regulations.

(d) A vessel engaged in fishing in close proximity to other vessels engaged in fishing may exhibit the additional signals described in Annex II to these Rules.

(e) A vessel when not engaged in fishing shall not exhibit the lights or shapes prescribed in this Rule, but only those prescribed for a vessel of her length.

| *Head on* | *Stern* | *Port* | *Day Shape* |
| | | | *Basket if under 20 meters* |

Vessel fishing—underway—making way

| *Head on* | *Stern* | *Port* | *Day shape* |

Vessel fishing with gear extending more than 150 meters—underway—making way

Rule 27. Vessels Not Under Command or Restricted in Their Ability to Maneuver

(a) A vessel not under command shall exhibit:

(i) two all-round red lights in a vertical line where they can best be seen;

(ii) two balls or similar shapes in a vertical line where they can best be seen;

(iii) when making way through the water, in addition to the lights prescribed in this paragraph, sidelights and a sternlight.

(b) A vessel restricted in her ability to maneuver, except a vessel engaged in mineclearance operations shall exhibit:

(i) three all-round lights in a vertical line where they can best be seen. The highest and lowest of these lights shall be red and the middle light shall be white;

(ii) three shapes in a vertical line where they can best be seen. The highest and lowest of the shapes shall be balls and the middle one a diamond;

(iii) when making way through the water, a masthead light or lights, sidelights and a sternlight, in addition to the lights prescribed in subparagraph (i);

(iv) when at anchor, in addition to the lights or shapes prescribed in subparagraphs (i) and (ii), the light, lights or shape prescribed in Rule 30.

(c) A power-driven vessel engaged in a towing operation such as severely restricts the

(iii) when making way through the water, masthead lights, sidelights and a sternlight, in addition to the lights prescribed in subparagraph (b) (i); and

(iv) when at anchor, in addition to the lights or shapes prescribed in subparagraphs (b) (i) and (ii), the light, lights or shapes prescribed in Rule 30.

(c) A vessel engaged in a towing operation which severely restricts the towing vessel

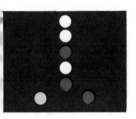  

Head on	*Stern*	*Port*	*Day shape*

Vessel not under command, making way

 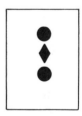

Head on	*Stern*	*Port*	*Day shape*

Vessel restricted in ability to maneuver, making way

towing vessel and her tow in their ability to deviate from their course shall, in addition to the lights or shapes prescribed in Rule 24 (a), exhibit the lights or shapes prescribed in sub-paragraph (b) *(i)* and *(ii)* of this Rule.

and her tow in their ability to deviate from their course shall, in addition to the lights or shapes prescribed in sub-paragraphs (b) *(i)* and *(ii)* of this Rule, exhibit the lights or shape prescribed in Rule 24.

(d) A vessel engaged in dredging or underwater operations, when restricted in her ability to maneuver, shall exhibit the lights and shapes prescribed in sub-paragraphs (b) *(i)*, *(ii)* and *(iii)* paragraph (b) of this Rule and shall in addition, when an obstruction exists, exhibit:

(i) two all-round red lights or two balls in a vertical line to indicate the side on which the obstruction exists;

(ii) two all-round green lights or two diamonds in a vertical line to indicate the side on which another vessel may pass;

(iii) when at anchor, the lights or shapes prescribed in this paragraph instead of the lights or shapes prescribed in Rule 30.

(iii) when at anchor, the lights or shape prescribed by this paragraph, instead of the lights or shapes prescribed in Rule 30 for anchored vessels.

(e) Whenever the size of a vessel engaged in diving operations makes it impracticable to exhibit all lights and shapes prescribed in paragraph (d) of this Rule, the following shall be exhibited:

(i) three all-round lights in a vertical line where they can best be seen. The highest and lowest of these lights shall be red and the middle light shall be white;

(ii) a rigid replica of the International Code flag "A" not less than 1 meter in height. Measures shall be taken to ensure all-round visibility.

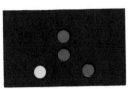
Head on

Stern

Port

Day shape

Vessel not under command, making way

Head on

Stern

Port

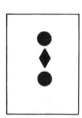
Day shape

Vessel restricted in ability to maneuver, making way

towing vessel and her tow in their ability to deviate from their course shall, in addition to the lights or shapes prescribed in Rule 24 (a), exhibit the lights or shapes prescribed in sub-paragraph (b) *(i)* and *(ii)* of this Rule.

and her tow in their ability to deviate from their course shall, in addition to the lights or shapes prescribed in sub-paragraphs (b) *(i)* and *(ii)* of this Rule, exhibit the lights or shape prescribed in Rule 24.

(d) A vessel engaged in dredging or underwater operations, when restricted in her ability to maneuver, shall exhibit the lights and shapes prescribed in sub-paragraphs (b) *(i)*, *(ii)* and *(iii)* paragraph (b) of this Rule and shall in addition, when an obstruction exists, exhibit:

(i) two all-round red lights or two balls in a vertical line to indicate the side on which the obstruction exists;

(ii) two all-round green lights or two diamonds in a vertical line to indicate the side on which another vessel may pass;

(iii) when at anchor, the lights or shapes prescribed in this paragraph instead of the lights or shapes prescribed in Rule 30.

(iii) when at anchor, the lights or shape prescribed by this paragraph, instead of the lights or shapes prescribed in Rule 30 for anchored vessels.

(e) Whenever the size of a vessel engaged in diving operations makes it impracticable to exhibit all lights and shapes prescribed in paragraph (d) of this Rule, the following shall be exhibited:

(i) three all-round lights in a vertical line where they can best be seen. The highest and lowest of these lights shall be red and the middle light shall be white;

(ii) a rigid replica of the International Code flag "A" not less than 1 meter in height. Measures shall be taken to ensure all-round visibility.

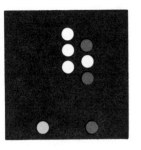

| *Head on* | *Stern* | *Port* | *Day shape* |

**Vessel towing—unable to deviate from course—less than 50 meters—
tow exceeds 200 meters astern**

Although Rule 27 (c) seems to limit its application to vessels towing astern (International), vessels towing alongside or pushing ahead may also show these signals. Therefore, if the vessel were towing alongside or pushing ahead on international waters, the towing light would not be carried. If on inland waters, she would show two towing lights instead of a sternlight. See discussion of Rule 3 (g) *(vi)*

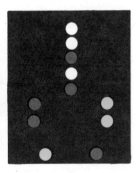

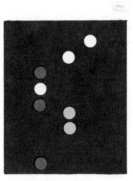

| *Head on* | *Stern* | *Port* | *Day shape* |

Vessel engaged in dredging or underwater operations

(f) A vessel engaged in mineclearance operations shall in addition to the lights prescribed for a power-driven vessel in Rule 23 or to the lights or shape prescribed for a vessel at anchor in Rule 30 as appropriate, exhibit three all-round green lights or three balls. One of these lights or shapes shall be exhibited near the foremast head and one at each end of the fore yard. These lights or shapes indicate that it is dangerous for another vessel to approach within 1,000 meters of the mineclearance vessel.

(g) Vessels of less than 12 meters in length, except those engaged in diving operations, shall not be required to exhibit the lights and shapes prescribed in this Rule.

(h) The signals prescribed in this Rule are not signals of vessels in distress and requiring assistance. Such signals are contained in Annex IV to these Regulations.

Rule 28. Vessels Constrained by Their Draft

A vessel constrained by her draft may, in addition to the lights prescribed for power-driven vessels in Rule 23, exhibit where they can best be seen three all-round red lights in a vertical line, or a cylinder.

(g) A vessel of less than 12 meters in length, except when engaged in diving operations, is not required to exhibit the lights or shapes prescribed in this Rule.

(h) The signals prescribed in this Rule are not signals of vessels in distress and requiring assistance. Such signals are contained in Annex IV to these Rules.

Rule 28.

(Reserved)

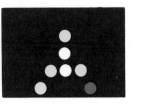  

| Head on | Stern | Port | Day shape |

Vessel engaged in mineclearance

Green lights are 32-point lights and may be seen from astern, depending on
the construction of the vessel

  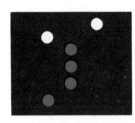 

| Head on | Stern | Port | Day shape |

Vessel constrained by draft (international waters only)

Rule 29. Pilot Vessels

(a) A vessel engaged on pilotage duty shall exhibit:

(i) at or near the masthead, two all-round lights in a vertical line, the upper being white and the lower red;

(ii) when underway, in addition, sidelights and a sternlight; and

(iii) when at anchor, in addition to the lights prescribed in subparagraph (i), the light, lights or shape prescribed in Rule 30 for vessels at anchor.

(b) A pilot vessel when not engaged on pilotage duty shall exhibit the lights or shapes prescribed for a similar vessel of her length.

(iii) when at anchor, in addition to the lights prescribed in subparagraph (i), the anchor light, lights, or shape prescribed in Rule 30 for anchored vessels.

(b) A pilot vessel when not engaged on pilotage duty shall exhibit the lights or shapes prescribed for a vessel of her length.

Rule 30. Anchored Vessels and Vessels Aground

(a) A vessel at anchor shall exhibit where it can best be seen:

(i) in the fore part, an all-round white light or one ball;

(ii) at or near the stern and at a lower level than the light prescribed in subparagraph (i), an all-round white light.

(b) A vessel of less than 50 meters in length may exhibit an all-round white light where it can best be seen instead of the lights prescribed in paragraph (a) of this Rule.

(c) A vessel at anchor may, and a vessel of 100 meters and more in length shall, also use the available working or equivalent lights to illuminate her decks.

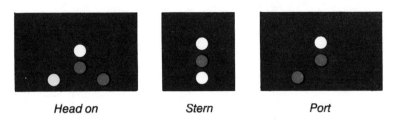

Head on   *Stern*   *Port*

Pilot vessel, underway

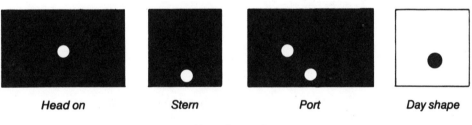

Head on   *Stern*   *Port*   *Day shape*

Vessel at anchor

(d) A vessel aground shall exhibit the lights prescribed in paragraph (a) or (b) of this Rule and in addition, where they can best be seen:

(i) two all-round red lights in a vertical line;

(ii) three balls in a vertical line.

(d) A vessel aground shall exhibit the lights prescribed in paragraph (a) or (b) of this Rule and in addition, if practicable, where they can best be seen:

(i) two all-round red lights in a vertical line; and

(ii) three balls in a vertical line.

(e) A vessel of less than 7 meters in length, when at anchor, not in or near a narrow channel, fairway or anchorage, or where other vessels normally navigate, shall not be required to exhibit the lights or shape prescribed in paragraphs (a) and (b) of this Rule.

(f) A vessel of less than 12 meters in length, when aground, shall not be required to exhibit the lights or shapes prescribed in subparagraphs (d) (i) and (ii) of this Rule.

(g) A vessel of less than 20 meters in length, when at anchor in a special anchorage area designated by the Secretary, shall not be required to exhibit the anchor lights and shapes required by this Rule.

Rule 31. Seaplanes

Where it is impracticable for a seaplane to exhibit lights and shapes of the characteristics or in the positions prescribed in the Rules of this Part she shall exhibit lights and shapes as closely similar in characteristics and position as is possible.

Head on

Stern

Port

Day shape

Vessel aground

PART D
SOUND AND LIGHT SIGNALS

Rule 32. Definitions

(a) The word "whistle" means any sound signalling appliance capable of producing the prescribed blasts and which complies with the specifications in Annex III to these Regulations.

(b) The term "short blast" means a blast of about one second's duration.

(c) The term "prolonged blast" means a blast of from four to six seconds' duration.

Rule 33. Equipment for Sound Signals

(a) A vessel of 12 meters or more in length shall be provided with a whistle and a bell and a vessel of 100 meters or more in length shall, in addition, be provided with a gong, the tone and sound of which cannot be confused with that of the bell. The whistle, bell and gong shall comply with the specifications in Annex III to these Regulations. The bell or gong or both may be replaced by other equipment having the same respective sound characteristics, provided that manual sounding of the prescribed signals shall always be possible.

(b) A vessel of less than 12 meters in length shall not be obliged to carry the sound signalling appliances prescribed in paragraph (a) of this Rule but if she does not, she shall be provided with some other means of making an efficient sound signal.

Rule 32.

The only whistle signals now contained in the Rules, Inland or International, are the short blast and the prolonged blast. No single blast of the whistle will be longer than six seconds in duration.

Rule 33.

With the passage of the Inland Rules, all vessels must have a means of making the required sound signals and there are no exemptions from this requirement. Small vessel operators should make sure that they obtain a suitable device for this purpose, such as a compressed air, or aerosol, horn.

For sound signal specifications the Rule refers to Annex III of the Rules where the frequencies of the whistles are given for various sizes of vessels. The lower the frequency, measured in Hertz (Hz), the deeper the tone of the whistle. If the vessels were singing in concert, the large vessels would sing bass (70-200 Hz), the medium-sized vessels would sing baritone (130-350 Hz) and the small vessels would sing tenor (250-700 Hz). For those not musically inclined, remember that, generally speaking, the deeper the tone of the whistle, the larger the vessel sounding it.

Annex III also gives the details of the bell and gong. These may be replaced by "other equipment," the Rule states, but it must have the same sound characteristics as those required by the Annex. Manual sounding of the signals must always be possible.

Rule 34. Maneuvering and Warning Signals

(a) When vessels are in sight of one another, a power-driven vessel underway, when maneuvering as authorized or required by these Rules, shall indicate that maneuver by the following signals on her whistle:

one short blast to mean "I am altering my course to starboard";

two short blasts to mean "I am altering my course to port" ;

three short blasts to mean "I am operating astern propulsion".

Rule 34. Maneuvering and Warning Signals

(a) When power-driven vessels are in sight of one another and meeting or crossing at a distance within half a mile of each other, each vessel underway, when maneuvering as authorized or required by these Rules:

(i) shall indicate that maneuver by the following signals on her whistle: one short blast to mean "I intend to leave you on my port side"; two short blasts to mean "I intend to leave you on my starboard side"; and three short blasts to mean "I am operating astern propulsion".

(ii) upon hearing the one or two blast signal of the other shall, if in agreement, sound the same whistle signal and take the steps necessary to effect a safe passing. If, however, from any cause, the vessel doubts the safety of the proposed maneuver, she shall sound the danger signal specified in paragraph (d) of this Rule and each vessel shall take appropriate precautionary action until a safe passing agreement is made.

Rule 34.

This Rule contains significant differences in requirements for signals, depending on whether you are operating on inland or international waters. The differences are as follows:

(1) Maneuvering signals under International Rules are signals of execution and indicate that a vessel is making a maneuver. They need not be answered. Maneuvering signals under Inland Rules are signals of intent (a proposal of what a vessel intends to do), and they must be answered by the other vessel, as an indication of agreement, before any maneuver can be executed.

(2) Although there is no distance mentioned in International Rules, in the Inland Rules signals need to be sounded only if the vessels will pass within half a mile of each other.

(3) Under International Rules, the whistle light must be a white light with a 5-mile visibility range and may be "repeated as appropriate." Under Inland Rules, the light is a white or yellow light with a 2-mile visibility range, and must be "synchronized with the whistle."

(4) Under International Rules, signals are provided for an overtaking situation in a narrow channel where the overtaken vessel has to take action to permit safe passage. There are no such special signals under Inland Rules.

(5) The Inland Rules provide for a signal of a prolonged blast when leaving a dock or berth but this signal is not in International Rules.

(6) In International waters, the maneuvering signals are signals of execution, and they must be sounded when a maneuver is executed. In inland waters, the signals indicate on which side one vessel intends to leave the other and do not indicate maneuvers. The Inland Rules now make provision for an agreement to be made by radiotelephone instead of sounding the whistle signals. This brings the Rules of the Road in line with what has been current practice. However, with regard to agreements made by radiotelephone the following should be noted:

i. *Always be certain* which vessel is making the agreement with you. There have been many instances of mistaken identity when using this handy device—the radiotelephone—some resulting in vehement *disagreement*.

(b) Any vessel may supplement the whistle signals prescribed in paragraph (a) of this Rule by light signals, repeated as appropriate, whilst the maneuver is being carried out:

(i) these light signals shall have the following significance:

one flash to mean "I am altering my course to starboard"; two flashes to mean "I am altering my course to port"; three flashes to mean "I am operating astern propulsion".

(ii) the duration of each flash shall be about one second, the interval between flashes shall be about one second, and the interval between successive signals shall be not less than ten seconds;

(iii) the light used for this signal shall, if fitted, be an all-round white light, visible at a minimum range of 5 miles, and shall comply with the provisions of Annex I to these Regulations.

(c) When in sight of one another in a narrow channel or fairway:

(i) a vessel intending to overtake another shall in compliance with Rule 9 (e) (i) indicate her intention by the following signals on her whistle:

two prolonged blasts followed by one short blast to mean

(b) A vessel may supplement the whistle signals prescribed in paragraph (a) of this Rule by light signals:

(i) These signals shall have the following significance: one flash to mean "I intend to leave you on my port side"; two flashes to mean "I intend to leave you on my starboard side"; three flashes to mean "I am operating astern propulsion";

(ii) The duration of each flash shall be about 1 second; and

(iii) The light used for this signal shall, if fitted, be one all-round white or yellow light, visible at a minimum range of 2 miles, synchronized with the whistle, and shall comply with the provisions of Annex I to these Rules.

(c) When in sight of one another:

(i) a power-driven vessel intending to overtake another power-driven vessel shall indicate her intention by the following signals on her whistle: one short blast to mean "I intend to overtake you on your

ii.   Always be certain what was said on the radiotelephone. Voices are often garbled and unclear. "Going too fast" may be heard as "meet on two blasts."

iii.   Always be certain that the other vessel is doing what he said he would do, or what you thought he said he would do. Keep a close eye on him. He may have told you he would "stop" when he only meant "stop engines."

iv.   Always be certain that you continue to monitor the radiotelephone after the agreement has been made. Something unexpected may develop and cause one or both of you to change your plans.

v.   Remember that the Rule says if agreement is not reached, whistle signals "shall be exchanged in a timely manner and shall prevail."

It should also be pointed out that the danger signal is the same under International and Inland Rules—at least five short and rapid blasts on the whistle. Its sounding is mandatory for any vessel approaching another when failing to understand the intentions of that vessel, or thinking that the vessel's action is not sufficient or appropriate.

The danger signal may also be sounded by a vessel at anchor. The only requirement for the signal is that the vessels be "in sight of one another [See Rule 34 (d)]. The rules consider the danger signal an "in sight signal," even though some have made arguments that it may be sounded in fog. If a watch officer knowledgeable in the rules heard a danger signal in fog, he would assume that there were two other vessels in the area that were in sight of one another. The vessel sounding the signal in fog would potentially be creating a very confusing and dangerous situation. He might well be held at fault if collision resulted. Officers would be well advised to use only proper fog signals in restricted visibility. Such signals will accomplish the desired effect of letting others know they are present, without interjecting complications.

Rule 34 (c) (international)—The requirements of this Rule are peculiar to the International Rules and provide for sound signals to be exchanged in narrow channels when one vessel is overtaking another. To provide these signals, the International Rules adopt the Inland Rules concept of " signals of intent." These signals are to be sounded "in compliance with Rule 9 (e) (*i*)," so they are to be sounded when "overtaking can take place only if the vessel to be overtaken has to take action to permit safe passing." The decision as to whether the vessel being overtaken will have to take action evidently is made by the overtaking vessel, for it is she who initiates the signals. If the vessel being overtaken is in doubt

"I intend to overtake you on your starboard side"; two prolonged blasts followed by two short blasts to mean "I intend to overtake you on your port side".

(ii) the vessel about to be overtaken when acting in accordance with Rule 9 (e) *(i)* shall indicate her agreement by the following signal on her whistle:

one prolonged, one short, one prolonged and one short blast, in that order.

(d) When vessels in sight of one another are approaching each other and from any cause either vessel fails to understand the intentions or actions of the other, or is in doubt whether sufficient action is being taken by the other to avoid collision, the vessel in doubt shall immediately indicate such doubt by giving at least five short and rapid blasts on the whistle. Such signal may be supplemented by a light signal of at least five short and rapid flashes.

(e) A vessel nearing a bend or an area of a channel or fairway where other vessels may be obscured by an intervening obstruction shall sound one prolonged blast. Such signal shall be answered with a prolonged blast by any approaching vessel that may be within

starboard side"; two short blasts to mean "I intend to overtake you on your port side"; and

(ii) the power-driven vessel about to be overtaken shall, if in agreement, sound a similar sound signal. If in doubt she shall sound the danger signal prescribed in paragraph (d).

(d) When vessels in sight of one another are approaching each other and from any cause either vessel fails to understand the intentions or actions of the other, or is in doubt whether sufficient action is being taken by the other to avoid collision, the vessel in doubt shall immediately indicate such doubt by giving at least five short and rapid blasts on the whistle. This signal may be supplemented by a light signal of at least five short and rapid flashes.

(e) A vessel nearing a bend or an area of a channel or fairway where other vessels may be obscured by an intervening obstruction shall sound one prolonged blast. This signal shall be answered with a prolonged blast by any approaching vessel that may be within

that the action is safe, or is not willing to take action as would be required by the proposed signal, she may (and should) sound the danger signal. Since this signal is optional, however, she may choose not to sound a signal, in which case the overtaking vessel should not attempt to pass. If the vessel being overtaken agrees to the maneuver, she will sound "a prolonged, a short, a prolonged, and a short blast, in that order." If the vessel being overtaken must change course to facilitate the other vessel's passage, she must sound the maneuvering signals given in Rule 34 (a), because these signals are to be sounded "when maneuvering as authorized or required by these Rules." It would be advisable to have frequent and open communication by radiotelephone during a maneuver such as this.

hearing around the bend or behind the intervening obstruction.

hearing around the bend or behind the intervening obstruction.

(f) If whistles are fitted on a vessel at a distance apart of more than 100 meters, one whistle only shall be used for giving maneuvering and warning signals.

(g) When a power-driven vessel is leaving a dock or berth, she shall sound one prolonged blast.

(h) A vessel that reaches agreement with another vessel in a meeting, crossing, or over-taking situation by using the radiotelephone as prescribed by the Bridge-to-Bridge Radio-telephone Act (85 Stat. 165; 33 U. S. C. 1207), is not obliged to sound the whistle signals prescribed by this Rule, but may do so. If agreement is not reached, then whistle signals shall be exchanged in a timely manner and shall prevail.

Rule 35. Sound Signals in Restricted Visibility

In or near an area of restricted visibility, whether by day or night, the signals prescribed in this Rule shall be as follows:

(a) A power-driven vessel making way through the water shall sound at intervals of not more than 2 minutes one prolonged blast.

(b) A power-driven vessel underway but stopped and making no way through the water shall sound at intervals of not more

(g) The Inland Rules state that a vessel leaving a dock or berth shall sound one prolonged blast. The International Rules do not state the same thing. However, a case may be made for giving this signal when moving from a dock, as it can be argued that the dock presents an "intervening obstruction" and the signal would be allowed under Rules 9 (f) and 34 (e). It does appear, however, that the intent of the International Rule is *not to require* the signal simply because a vessel is leaving a dock.

(h) 33CFR 26.04 (b) instructs an operator to use the radiotelephone to confirm his vessel's intentions.

Rule 35.

Fog signals are to be used when operating "in or *near* an area of restricted visibility." Since this phrase is used in Rule 19 of the Steering and Sailing Rules, you may wish to review the discussion of that Rule.

The question might come to mind as to how restricted the visibility must be for fog signals to be required. In other words, "How foggy is too foggy?" You note from the audibility table in Annex III of the International Rules that the range at which you can expect to hear the fog signal of a large vessel is about two miles. This might be increased slightly by existing meteorological conditions. If the prevailing visibility is two and a half miles or more, then you can probably be safe in assuming that sounding the fog signals will accomplish little more than the aggravation of the crew. If the range of visibility is less than the range of your whistle, you should certainly be sounding fog signals.

than 2 minutes two prolonged blasts in succession with an interval of about 2 seconds between them.

(c) A vessel not under command, a vessel restricted in her ability to maneuver, a vessel constrained by her draft, a sailing vessel, a vessel engaged in fishing and a vessel engaged in towing or pushing another vessel shall, instead of the signals prescribed in paragraphs (a) or (b) of this Rule, sound at intervals of not more than 2 minutes three blasts in succession, namely one prolonged followed by two short blasts.

(d) A vessel engaged in fishing, when at anchor, and a vessel restricted in her ability to maneuver when carrying out her work at anchor, shall instead of the signals prescribed in paragraph (g) of this Rule sound the signal prescribed in paragraph (c) of this Rule.

(e) A vessel towed or if more than one vessel is towed the last vessel of the tow, if manned, shall at intervals of not more than 2 minutes sound four blasts in succession, namely one prolonged followed by three short blasts. When practicable, this signal shall be made immediately after the signal made by the towing vessel.

(c) A vessel not under command; a vessel restricted in her ability to maneuver, whether underway or at anchor; a sailing vessel; a vessel engaged in fishing, whether underway or at anchor; and a vessel engaged in towing or pushing another vessel shall, instead of the signals prescribed in paragraphs (a) or (b) of this Rule, sound at intervals of not more than 2 minutes, three blasts in succession; namely one prolonged followed by two short blasts.

(d) A vessel towed or if more than one vessel is towed the last vessel of the tow, if manned, shall at intervals of not more than 2 minutes sound four blasts in succession; namely, one prolonged followed by three short blasts. When practicable, this signal shall be made immediately after the signal made by the towing vessel.

Although worded differently, both sets of Rules require that vessels engaged in fishing, and vessels restricted in their ability to maneuver, do not sound the regular anchor signals that apply to other vessels. These vessels sound the same signal (one prolonged and two short blasts) whether underway or at anchor.

(f) When a pushing vessel and a vessel being pushed ahead are rigidly connected in a composite unit they shall be regarded as a power-driven vessel and shall give the signals prescribed in paragraphs (a) or (b) of this Rule.

(g) A vessel at anchor shall at intervals of not more than one minute ring the bell rapidly for about 5 seconds. In a vessel of 100 meters or more in length the bell shall be sounded in the forepart of the vessel and immediately after the ringing of the bell the gong shall be sounded rapidly for about 5 seconds in the after part of the vessel. A vessel at anchor may in addition sound three blasts in succession, namely one short, one prolonged and one short blast, to give warning of her position and of the possibility of collision to an approaching vessel.

(h) A vessel aground shall give the bell signal and if required the gong signal prescribed in paragraph (f) of this Rule and shall, in addition, give three separate and distinct strokes on the bell immediately before and after the rapid ringing of the bell. A vessel aground may in addition sound an appropriate whistle signal.

(i) A vessel of less than 12 meters in length shall not be obliged to give the above-mentioned signals but, if she does

(e) When a pushing vessel and a vessel being pushed ahead are rigidly connected in a composite unit they shall be regarded as a power-driven vessel and shall give the signals prescribed in paragraphs (a) or (b) of this Rule.

(f) A vessel at anchor shall at intervals of not more than 1 minute ring the bell rapidly for about 5 seconds. In a vessel of 100 meters or more in length the bell shall be sounded in the forepart of the vessel and immediately after the ringing of the bell the gong shall be sounded rapidly for about 5 seconds in the after part of the vessel. A vessel at anchor may in addition sound three blasts in succession; namely, one short, one prolonged and one short blast, to give warning of her position and of the possibility of collision to an approaching vessel.

(g) A vessel aground shall give the bell signal and if required the gong signal prescribed in paragraph (f) of this Rule and shall, in addition, give three separate and distinct strokes on the bell immediately before and after the rapid ringing of the bell. A vessel aground may in addition sound an appropriate whistle signal.

(h) A vessel of less than 12 meters in length shall not be obliged to give the above-mentioned signals but, if she does

Paragraph (e) (Inland) or (f) (International) of the Rule is addressed to vessels connected in a composite unit. A composite unit defined by the Coast Guard is as follows:

33 CFR 88.3 pushing vessel and vessel being pushed: Composite unit. Rule 24 (b) of the 72 COLREGS states that when a pushing vessel and a vessel being pushed ahead are rigidly connected in a composite unit, they are regarded as a power-driven vessel and must exhibit the lights under Rule 23. A "composite unit" is interpreted to be a pushing vessel that is rigidly connected by mechanical means to a vessel being pushed so they react to sea and swell as one vessel. "Mechanical means" does not include the following:

(a) Lines.   (c) Wires.

(b) Hawsers.   (d) Chains.

As you read paragraph (f) (Inland) or (g) (International) of the Rule, you might be tempted to think that any vessel at anchor would sound these signals, but this is not the case. A fishing vessel or a vessel restricted in her ability to maneuver sounds the same signal underway or at anchor, but the other vessels listed in paragraph (c) (sailing vessel, towing vessel, etc.) presumably sound the anchor signal given here. Of course this means that some anchored vessels sound their fog signals at two-minute intervals (paragraph (c)) and some at one-minute intervals (paragraph (f) (g)).

As already mentioned small vessels must carry a means of making the required sound signals. This is reinforced in paragraph (h) (Inland) or (i) (International) which requires vessels even less than twelve meters in length to make the required signals or "some other efficient sound signal."

The Rules provide an identity signal of four short blasts for pilot vessels engaged on pilotage duty. All commentators on the subject seem convinced that this Rule extends the identification signal for a power-driven pilot vessel to all pilot vessels. We realize that there are not many sail pilot vessels in our waters, but just on the chance that there may some day be one, let us see if she could sound an identity signal under this Rule. The Rule states that a vessel may sound the signal "in addition to the signals prescribed in paragraphs (a), (b) or (f)" [(g) in International], and paragraphs (a) and (b), contain signals which can only be sounded by power-driven vessels. The signals set forth in paragraph (f) [(g) in International] can only be sounded by a vessel at anchor. A sailing vessel "shall" sound the signal in paragraph (c). It is not optional. Therefore, the conclusion seems to be that a sail pilot vessel underway is not allowed, by the present Rules, to sound an identity signal, because she is not allowed to sound any of the prerequisite signals.

not, shall make some other efficient sound signal at intervals of not more than 2 minutes.

(j) A pilot vessel when engaged on pilotage duty may in addition to the signals prescribed in paragraphs (a), (b) or (g) of this Rule sound an identity signal consisting of four short blasts.

not, shall make some other efficient sound signal at intervals of not more than 2 minutes.

(i) A pilot vessel when engaged on pilotage duty may in addition to the signals prescribed in paragraphs (a), (b) or (f) of this Rule sound an identity signal consisting of four short blasts.

(j) The following vessels shall not be required to sound signals as prescribed in paragraph (f) of this Rule when anchored in a special anchorage area designated by the Secretary:

(i) a vessel of less than 20 meters in length; and

(ii) a barge, canal boat, scow, or other nondescript craft.

Rule 36. Signals to Attract Attention

If necessary to attract the attention of another vessel, any vessel may make light or sound signals that cannot be mistaken for any signal authorized elsewhere in these Rules, or may direct the beam of her searchlight in the direction of the danger, in such a way as not to embarrass any vessel. Any light to attract the attention of another vessel shall be such that it cannot be mistaken for any aid to navigation. For the purpose of this Rule the use of high intensity intermittent or revolving lights, such as strobe lights, shall be avoided.

Rule 36. Signals to Attract Attention

If necessary to attract the attention of another vessel, any vessel may make light or sound signals that cannot be mistaken for any signal authorized elsewhere in these Rules, or may direct the beam of her searchlight in the direction of the danger, in such a way as not to embarrass any vessel.

Rule 36.

According to this Rule if you must attract the attention of another vessel, you may use light or sound signals, as long as these signals cannot be confused with required signals. You may also direct the beam of a searchlight in the direction of danger, "in such a way as not to embarrass any vessel." The word embarrass can mean any of the following:

1. To beset with difficulties
2. To impede
3. To complicate

If a vessel has to cross the path of your searchlight, the chances are good that the light will cause vision "difficulties" for the look-outs and bridge watches of other vessels, thereby "impeding" the safe passage of such vessels and "complicating" their navigation. You should be sure, then, that the beam of any light employed in such a situation will not have such adverse effects.

Rule 37. Distress Signals

When a vessel is in distress and requires assistance she shall use or exhibit the signals described in Annex IV to these Regulations.

PART E
EXEMPTIONS

Rule 38. Exemptions

Any vessel (or class of vessels) provided that she complies with the requirements of the International Regulations for Preventing Collisions at Sea, 1960, the keel of which is laid or which is at a corresponding stage of construction before the entry into force of these Regulations may be exempted from compliance therewith as follows:

(a) The installation of lights with ranges prescribed in Rule 22, until four years after the date of entry into force of these Regulations.

(b) The installation of lights with color specifications as prescribed in Section 7 of Annex I to these Regulations, until four years after the date of entry into force of these Regulations.

(c) The repositioning of lights as a result of conversion from Imperial to metric units and rounding off measurement figures, permanent exemption.

(d)   *(i)* The repositioning of masthead lights on vessels of less than 150 meters in length,

Rule 38. Exemptions

Any vessel or class of vessels, the keel of which is laid or which is at a corresponding stage of construction before the date of enactment of this Act, provided that she complies with the requirements of—

(a) The Act of June 7, 1897 (30 Stat. 96), as amended (33 U.S.C. 154-232) for vessels navigating the waters subject to that statute;

(b) Section 4233 of the Revised Statutes (33 U.S.C. 301-356) for vessels navigating the waters subject to that statute;

(c) The Act of February 8, 1895 (28 Stat. 645), as amended (33 U.S.C. 241-295) for vessels navigating the waters subject to that statute; or

(d) Sections 3, 4, and 5 of the Act of April 25, 1940 (54 Stat. 163), as amended (46 U.S.C.

resulting from the prescriptions of Section 3 (a) of Annex I to these Regulations, permanent exemption.

(ii) The repositioning of masthead lights on vessels of 150 meters or more in length, resulting from the prescriptions of Section 3 (a) of Annex I to these Regulations, until 9 years after the date of entry into force of these Regulations.

526 b, c, and d) for motorboats navigating the waters subject to that statute: shall be exempted from compliance with the technical Annexes to these Rules as follows:

(i) the installation of lights with ranges prescribed in Rule 22, until 4 years after the effective date of these Rules, except that vessels of less than 20 meters in length are permanently exempt;

(ii) the installation of lights with color specifications as prescribed in Annex I to these Rules, until 4 years after the effective date of these Rules, except that vessels of less than 20 meters in length are permanently exempt:

(iii) the repositioning of lights as a result of conversion to metric units and rounding off measurement figures, are permanently exempt; and

(iv) the horizontal repositioning of masthead lights prescribed by Annex I to these Rules:

(1) on vessels of less than 150 meters in length, permanent exemption.

(2) on vessels of 150 meters or more in length, until 9 years after the effective date of these Rules.

(v) the restructuring or repositioning of all lights to meet the prescriptions of Annex I to these Rules, until 9 years

after the effective date of these Rules;

(vi) power-driven vessels of 12 meters or more but less than 20 meters in length are permanently exempt from the provisions of Rule 23 (a) *(i)* and 23 (a) *(iv)* provided that, in place of these lights, the vessel exhibits a white light aft visible all round the horizon; and

(vii) the requirements for sound signal appliances prescribed in Annex IIII to these Rules, until 9 years after the effective date of these Rules.

(e) The repositioning of masthead lights resulting from the prescriptions of Section 2 (b) of Annex I to these Regulations, until 9 years after the date of entry into force of these Regulations.

(f) The repositioning of sidelights resulting from the prescriptions of Sections 2 (g) and 3 (b) of Annex I to these Regulations, until 9 years after the date of entry into force of these Regulations.

(g) The requirements for sound signal appliances prescribed in Annex III to these Regulations, until 9 years after the date of entry into force of these Regulations.

(h) The repositioning of all-round lights resulting from the prescription of Section 9 (b) of Annex I to these Regulations, permanent exemption.

Sec. 3. The Secretary may issue regulations necessary to implement and interpret this Act. The Secretary shall establish the following technical annexes to the Rules: Annex I, Positioning and Technical Details of Lights and Shapes; Annex II, Additional Signals for Fishing Vessels Fishing in Close Proximity; Annex III, Technical Details of Sound Appliances; and Annex IV, Distress Signals. These annexes shall be as consistent as possible with the respective annexes to the International Regulations. The Secretary may establish other technical annexes, including local pilot rules.

Sec. 4. (a) Whoever operates a vessel in violation of this Act, or of any regulation issued thereunder, or in violation of a certificate of alternative compliance issued under Rule 1 is liable to a civil penalty of not more than $5,000 for each violation.

(b) Every vessel subject to this Act, other than a public vessel being used for noncommercial purposes, that is operated in violation of this Act, or of any regulation issued thereunder, or in violation of a certificate of alternative compliance issued under Rule 1 is liable to a civil penalty of not more than $5,000 for each violation, for which penalty the vessel may be seized and proceeded

against in the district court of the United States of any district within which the vessel may be found.

(c) The Secretary may assess any civil penalty authorized by this section. No such penalty may be assessed until the person charged, or the owner of the vessel charged, as appropriate, shall have been given notice of the violation involved and an opportunity for a hearing. For good cause shown, the Secretary may remit, mitigate, or compromise any penalty assessed. Upon the failure of the person charged, or the owner of the vessel charged, to pay an assessed penalty, as it may have been mitigated or compromised, the Secretary may request the Attorney General to commence an action in the appropriate district court of the United States for collection of the penalty as assessed, without regard to the amount involved, together with such other relief as may be appropriate.

(d) The Secretary of the Treasury shall withhold or revoke, at the request of the Secretary, the clearance, required by section 4197 of the Revised Statutes of the United States (46 U. S. C. 91) of any vessel, the owner or operator of which is subject to any of the penalties in this section. Clearance may be granted in

such cases upon the filing of a
bond or other surety satisfactory to the Secretary.

Sec. 5. (a) The Secretary shall
establish a Rules of the Road
Advisory Council (hereinafter
referred to as the Council) not
exceeding 21 members. To as-
sure balanced representation,
members shall be chosen, in-
sofar as practical from the following groups: (1) recognized
experts and leaders in organiza-
tions having an active interest
in the Rules of the Road and
vessel and port safety, (2) repre-
sentatives of owners and
operators of vessels, professional mariners, recreational
beaters, and the recreational
boating industry, (3) individuals
with an interest in maritime
law, and (4) Federal and State
officials with responsibility for
vessel and port safety. Additional persons may be appointed to
panels of the Council to assist
the Council in the performance
of its functions.

(b) The Council shall
advise, consult with, and make
recommendations to the Secretary on matters relating to any
major proposals for changes to
the Inland Rules. The Council
may recommend changes to the
Inland Rules and International
Regulations to the Secretary.
Any advice or recommendation
made by the Council to the

Secretary shall reflect the independent judgment of the Council on the matter concerned. The Council shall meet at the call of the Secretary, but in any event not less than once during each calendar year. All proceedings of the Council shall be public, and a record of the proceedings shall be made available for public inspection.

(c) The Secretary shall furnish to the Council an executive secretary and such secretarial, clerical, and other services as are deemed necessary for the conduct of its business. Members of the Council who are not officers or employees of the United States shall, while attending meetings of the Council or while otherwise engaged in the business of the Council, be entitled to receive compensation at a rate fixed by the Secretary, not exceeding the daily equivalent of the current rate of basic pay in effect for GS-18 of the General Schedule under section 5332 of title 5, United States Code, including travel time, and while away from their home or regular place of business, they may be allowed travel expenses, including per diem in lieu of subsistence, as authorized by section 5703 of title 5, United States Code. Payments under this section shall not render members

of the Council officers or
employees of the United States
for any purpose.

(d) Unless extended
by subsequent Act of Congress,
the Council shall terminate
five years from the date of enactment of this Act.

Sec. 6. The International
Navigational Rules Act of 1977
(91 Stat. 308; 33 U. S. C. 1601),
is amended as follows:

(1) in section 5 by
amending subsection (a) to
read as follows:

"The International Regu-
lations do not apply to vessels
while in waters of the United
States shoreward of the navigational demarcation lines
dividing the high seas from
harbors, rivers, and other inland waters of the United
States.";

(2) in section 6, by
adding a new subsection (d) as
follows:

"(d) A certification authorized by this section may be
issued for a class of vessels.";

(3) in subsection (a)
of section 9 by striking "$500"
and inserting in lieu thereof
$5,000".

(4) in subsection (b) of
section (b) of section 9 by striking "$500" and inserting in lieu
thereof "not more than $5,000".

Sec. 7. Sections 2, 4, 6(1) and 8 (a) are effective twelve months after the date of enactment of this Act, except that on the Great Lakes, the effective date of sections 2 and 4 will be established by the Secretary. Section 5 is effective October 1, 1981.

Sec. 8. (a) The laws specified in the following schedules are repealed. Any prior rights or liabilities existing under these laws are not affected by their repeal.

REVISED STATUTES

Sec. 4233.
Sec. 4233A.
Sec. 4233B.
Sec. 4233C.

TABLE OF REVISED STATUTES UNDER RULE 38 INLAND RULES

Date	Chapter	Statutes at Large Sections	Volume	Page
1890: Aug. 19	802	—	26	320
1893: Mar. 3	202	—	27	557
1895: Feb. 19	102	1, 4	28	672
1897: Mar. 3	889	5, 12, 13	29	689
1897: June 7	4	—	30	96
1900: Feb. 19	22	—	31	30
1905: Mar. 3	1457	10	33	1032
1914: May 25	98	—	38	381
1933: Mar. 1	157	—	47	1417
1935: Aug. 21	595	2, 3, 4, 5	49	669
1936: May 20	433	—	49	1367
1940: Apr. 22	128	1, 3	54	150
Apr. 25	155	3, 4, 5	54	164
1945: Dec. 3	511	1, 2	59	590
1948: Mar. 5	99	—	62	69
May 21	328	—	62	249
1953: Aug. 8	386	—	67	497
1956: June 4	353	—	70	228
1958:	Public Law			
Aug. 14	85-635	—	72	590
Aug. 14	85-656	—	72	612
1963: Aug. 5	88-84	—	77	116
Oct. 30	88-163	—	77	281
1966: Nov. 5	89-764	1, 2, 5, 6	80	1313

(b) The following
laws are repealed when the
Secretary establishes an effective date under section 7.

Date	Chapter	Statutes at Large Sections	Volume	Page
1895: Feb. 8	64	—	28	645
1928: May 17	600	—	45	592
May 17	601	—	45	593
1929: Feb. 28	370	—	45	1405
1932: May 9	175	—	47	152
1940: Apr. 22	128	2	54	150
1948: Mar. 18	138	—	62	82
	Public Law			
1958: Mar. 28	85-350	—	72	49
1966: Nov. 5	89-764	3, 4	80	1313

Sec. 9. Section 2 (c) of the Act
of February 19, 1895 (28 Stat.
672), as amended (33 U. S. C.
151), is amended by striking the
words "the Canal Zone,".

ANNEXES

The Annexes to both sets of Rules are included in this volume. The Pilot Rules are Annex V to the Inland Rules.

ANNEX I: POSITIONING AND TECHNICAL
DETAILS OF LIGHTS AND SHAPES

1. Definition

The term "height above the hull" means height above the upper-most continuous deck. This height shall be measured from the position vertically beneath the location of the light.

2. Vertical positioning and spacing of lights

(a) On a power-driven vessel of 20 meters or more in length the masthead lights shall be placed as follows:

(i) the forward masthead light, or if only one masthead light is carried, then that light, at a height above the hull of not less than 6 meters, and, if the breadth of the vessel exceeds 6 meters, then at a height above the hull not less than such breadth, so however that the light need not be placed at a greater height above the hull than 12 meters;

(ii) when two masthead lights are carried the after one shall be at least 4.5 meters vertically higher than the forward one.

(b) The vertical separation of masthead lights of power-driven vessels shall be such that in all normal conditions of trim the after light will be seen over and separate from the forward light at a distance of 1000 meters from the stem when viewed from sea level.

(c) The masthead light of a power-driven vessel of 12 meters but less than 20 meters in length shall be placed at a height above the gunwale of not less than 2.5 meters.

(d) A power-driven vessel of less than 12 meters in length may carry the uppermost light at a height of less than 2.5 meters above the gunwale. When however a masthead light is carried in addition

ANNEX I: POSITIONING AND TECHNICAL DETAILS OF LIGHTS AND SHAPES

§ 84.01 Definitions

(a) The term "height above the hull" means height above the uppermost continuous deck. This height shall be measured from the position vertically beneath the location of the light.

(b) The term "practical cut-off" means, for vessels 20 meters or more in length, 12.5 percent of the minimum luminous intensity (Table 84.15 (b)) corresponding to the greatest range of visibility for which the requirements of Annex I are met.

(c) The term "Rule" or "Rules" means the Inland Navigation Rules contained in Sec. 2 of the Inland Navigation Rules Act of 1980 (Pub. L. 96-591, 94 Stat. 3415, 33 U.S.C. 2001, December 24, 1980) as amended.

§ 84.03 Vertical positioning and spacing of lights

(a) On a power-driven vessel of 20 meters or more in length the masthead lights shall be placed as follows:

(1) The forward masthead light, or if only one masthead light is carried, then that light, at a height above the hull of not less than 5 meters, and, if the breadth of the vessel exceeds 5 meters, then at a height above the hull not less than such breadth, so however that the light need not be placed at a greater height above the hull than 8 meters;

(2) When two masthead lights are carried the after one shall be at least 2 meters vertically higher than the forward one.

(b) The vertical separation of the masthead lights of power-driven vessels shall be such that in all normal conditions of trim the after light will be seen over and separate from the forward light at a distance of 1000 meters from the stem when viewed from water level.

(c) The masthead light of a power-driven vessel of 12 meters but less than 20 meters in length shall be placed at a height above the gunwale of not less than 2.5 meters.

(d) The masthead light, or the all-round light described in Rule 23 (c), of a power-driven vessel of less than 12 meters in length shall be carried at least one meter higher than the sidelights.

to sidelights and a sternlight or the all-round light prescribed in Rule 23 (c) *(i)* is carried in addition to sidelights, then such masthead light or all-round light shall be carried at least 1 meter higher than the sidelights.

(e) One of the two or three masthead lights prescribed for a power-driven vessel when engaged in towing or pushing another vessel shall be placed in the same position as either the forward masthead light or the after masthead light; provided that, if carried on the aftermast, the lowest after masthead light shall be at least 4.5 meters vertically higher than the forward masthead light.

(f) *(i)* The masthead light or lights prescribed in Rule 23 (a) shall be so placed as to be above and clear of all other lights and obstructions except as described in subparagraph *(ii)*.

(ii) When it is impracticable to carry the all-round lights prescribed by Rule 27 (b) *(i)* or Rule 28 below the masthead lights, they may be carried above the after masthead light(s) or vertically in between the forward masthead light(s) and after masthead light(s), provided that in the latter case the requirement of Section 3 (c) of this Annex shall be complied with.

(g) The sidelights of a power-driven vessel shall be placed at a height above the hull not greater than three quarters of that of the forward masthead light. They shall not be so low as to be interfered with by deck lights.

(h) The sidelights, if in a combined lantern and carried on a power-driven vessel of less than 20 meters in length, shall be placed not less than 1 meter below the masthead light.

(i) When the Rules prescribe two or three lights to be carried in a vertical line, they shall be spaced as follows:

(i) on a vessel of 20 meters in length or more such lights shall be spaced not less than 2 meters apart, and the lowest of these lights shall, except where a towing light is required, be placed at a height of not less than 4 meters above the hull;

(ii) on a vessel of less than 20 meters in length such lights shall be spaced not less than 1 meter apart and the lowest of these lights shall, except where a towing light is required, be placed at a height of not less than 2 meters above the gunwale;

(iii) when three lights are carried they shall be equally spaced.

(j) The lower of the two all-round lights prescribed for a vessel when engaged in fishing shall be at a height above the sidelights not less than twice the distance between the two vertical lights.

(e) One of the two or three masthead lights prescribed for a power-driven vessel when engaged in towing or pushing another vessel shall be placed in the same position as either the forward masthead light or the after masthead light, provided that the lowest after masthead light shall be at least 2 meters vertically higher than the forward masthead light.

(f) (1) The masthead light or lights prescribed in Rule 23 (a) shall be so placed as to be above and clear of all other lights and obstructions except as described in subparagraph (f) (2) of this section.

(2) When it is impracticable to carry the all-round lights prescribed in Rule 27 (b) *(i)* below the masthead lights, they may be carried above the after masthead light(s) or vertically in between the forward masthead light(s) and after masthead light(s), provided that in the latter case the requirement of § 84.05 (d) shall be complied with.

(g) The sidelights of a power-driven vessel shall be placed at least one meter lower than the forward masthead light. They shall not be so low as to be interfered with by deck lights.

(h) [Reserved]

(i) When the Rules prescribe two or three lights to be carried in a vertical line, they shall be spaced as follows:

(1) On a vessel of 20 meters in length or more such lights shall be spaced not less than 1 meter apart, and the lowest of these lights shall, except where a towing light is required, be placed at a height of not less than 4 meters above the hull;

(2) On a vessel of less than 20 meters in length such lights shall be spaced not less than 1 meter apart and the lowest of these lights shall, except where towing light is required, be placed at a height of not less than 2 meters above the gunwale;

(3) When three lights are carried they shall be equally spaced.

(j) The lower of the two all-round lights prescribed for a vessel when engaged in fishing shall be at a height above the sidelights not less than twice the distance between the two vertical lights.

(k) The forward anchor light prescribed in Rule 30 (a) *(i)*, when two are carried, shall not be less than 4.5 meters above the after one.

On a vessel of 50 meters or more in length this forward anchor light shall be placed at a height of not less than 6 meters above the hull.

3. Horizontal positioning and spacing of lights

(a) When two masthead lights are prescribed for a power-driven vessel, the horizontal distance between them shall not be less than one half of the length of the vessel but need not be more than 100 meters.

The forward light shall be placed not more than one quarter of the length of the vessel from the stem.

(b) On a power-driven vessel of 20 meters or more in length the sidelights shall not be placed in front of the forward masthead lights. They shall be placed at or near the side of the vessel.

(c) When the lights prescribed in Rule 27 (b) *(i)* or Rule 28 are placed vertically between the forward masthead light(s) and the after masthead light(s) these all-round lights shall be placed at a horizontal distance of not less than 2 meters from the fore and aft centerline of the vessel in the athwartship direction.

4. Details of location of direction-indicating lights for fishing vessels, dredgers and vessels engaged in underwater operations

(a) The light indicating the direction of the outlying gear from a vessel engaged in fishing as prescribed in Rule 26 (c) *(ii)* shall be placed at a horizontal distance of not less than 2 meters and not more than 6 meters away from the two all-round red and white lights. This light shall be placed not higher than the all-round white light prescribed in Rule 26 (c) *(i)* and not lower than the sidelights.

(b) The lights and shapes on a vessel engaged in dredging or underwater operations to indicate the obstructed side and/or the side on which it is safe to pass, as prescribed in Rule 27 (d) *(i)* and *(ii)*, shall be placed at the maximum practical horizontal distance, but in no case less than 2 meters, from the lights or shapes prescribed in 27 (b) *(i)* and *(ii)*. In no case shall the upper of these lights or shapes be at a greater height than the lower of the three lights or shapes prescribed in Rule 27 (b) *(i)* and *(ii)*.

(k) The forward anchor light prescribed in Rule 30 (a) *(i)*, when two are carried, shall not be less than 4.5 meters above the after one.

On a vessel of 50 meters or less in length this forward anchor light shall be placed at a height of not less than 6 meters above the hull.

§ 84.05   Horizontal positioning and spacing of lights

(a) Except as specified in paragraph (b) of this section, when two masthead lights are prescribed for a power-driven vessel, the horizontal distance between them shall not be less than one quarter of the length of the vessel but need not be more than 50 meters. The forward light shall be placed not more than one half of the length of the vessel from the stem.

(b) On power-driven vessels 50 meters but less than 60 meters in length operated on the Western Rivers, the horizontal distance between masthead lights shall not be less than 10 meters.

(c) On a power-driven vessel of 20 meters or more in length the sidelights shall not be placed in front of the forward masthead lights. They shall be placed at or near the side of the vessel.

(d) When the lights prescribed in Rule 27 (b) *(i)* are placed vertically between the forward masthead light(s) and the after masthead light(s) these all-round lights shall be placed at a horizontal distance of not less than 2 meters from the fore and aft centerline of the vessel in the athwartship direction.

§ 84.07   Details of location of direction-indicating lights for fishing vessels, dredgers and vessels engaged in underwater operations

(a) The light indicating the direction of the outlying gear from a vessel engaged in fishing as prescribed in Rule 26 (c) *(ii)* shall be placed at a horizontal distance of not less than 2 meters and not more than 6 meters away from the two all-round red and white lights. This light shall be placed not higher than the all-round white light prescribed in Rule 26 (c) *(i)* and not lower than the sidelights.

(b) The lights and shapes on a vessel engaged in dredging or underwater operations to indicate the obstructed side and/or the side on which it is safe to pass, as prescribed in Rule 27 (d) *(i)* and *(ii)*, shall be placed at the maximum practical horizontal distance, but in no case less than 2 meters, from the lights or shapes prescribed in Rule 27 (b) *(i)* and *(ii)*. In no case shall the upper of these lights or shapes be at a greater height than the lower of the three lights or shapes prescribed in Rule 27 (b) *(i)* and *(ii)*.

5. Screens for sidelights

The sidelights of vessels of 20 meters or more in length shall be fitted with inboard screens painted matt black, and meeting the requirements of Section 9 of this Annex. On vessels of less than 20 meters in length the sidelights, if necessary to meet the requirements of Section 9 of this Annex, shall be fitted with inboard matt black screens. With a combined lantern, using a single vertical filament and a very narrow division between the green and red sections, external screens need not be fitted.

6. Shapes

(a) Shapes shall be black and of the following sizes:
   (i) a ball shall have a diameter of not less than 0.6 meter;
   (ii) a cone shall have a base diameter of not less than 0.6 meter and a height equal to its diameter;
   (iii) a cylinder shall have a diameter of at least 0.6 meter and a height of twice its diameter;
   (iv) a diamond shape shall consist of two cones as defined in (ii) above having a common base.

(b) The vertical distance between shapes shall be at least 1.5 meter.

(c) In a vessel of less than 20 meters in length shapes of lesser dimensions but commensurate with the size of the vessel may be used and the distance apart may be correspondingly reduced.

7. Color specification of lights

The chromaticity of all navigation lights shall conform to the following standards, which lie within the boundaries of the area of the diagram specified for each color by the International Commission on Illumination (CIE).

§ 84.09   Screens

(a) The sidelights of vessels of 20 meters or more in length shall be fitted with mat black inboard screens and meet the requirements of § 84.17. On vessels of less than 20 meters in length the sidelights, if necessary to meet the requirements of § 84.17, shall be fitted with mat black inboard screens. With a combined lantern, using a single vertical filament and a very narrow division between the green and red sections, external screens need not be fitted.

(b) On power-driven vessels less than 12 meters in length constructed after July 31, 1983, the masthead light, or the all-round light described in Rule 23 (c) shall be screened to prevent direct illumination of the vessel forward of the operator's position.

§ 84.11   Shapes

(a) Shapes shall be black and of the following sizes:
(1) a ball shall have a diameter of not less than 0.6 meter;
(2) a cone shall have a base diameter of not less than 0.6 meter and a height equal to its diameter;
(3) a diamond shape shall consist of two cones (as defined in paragraph (a) (2) of this section) having a common base.

(b) The vertical distance between shapes shall be at least 1.5 meter.
(c) In a vessel of less than 20 meters in length shapes of lesser dimensions but commensurate with the size of the vessel may be used and the distance apart may be correspondingly reduced.

§ 84.13   Color specification of lights

The chromaticity of all navigation lights shall conform to the following standards, which lie within the boundaries of the area of the diagram specified for each color by the International Commission on Illumination (CIE), in the "Colors of Light Signals", which is incorporated by reference. It is Publication CIE No. 2.2. (TC-1.6), 1975, and is available from the Illumination Engineering Society, 345 East 47th Street, New York, NY 10017. It is also available for inspection at the Office of the Federal Register, Room 8401, 1100 L Street N.W., Washington, D.C. 20408. This incorporation by reference was approved by the Director of the Federal Register.

The boundaries of the area for each color are given by indicating the corner coordinates, which are as follows:

   (i) White:

x	0.525	0.525	0.452	0.310	0.310	0.443
y	0.382	0.440	0.440	0.348	0.283	0.382

   (ii) Green:

x	0.028	0.009	0.300	0.203
y	0.385	0.723	0.511	0.356

  (iii) Red:

x	0.680	0.660	0.735	0.721
y	0.320	0.320	0.265	0.259

  (iv) Yellow:

x	0.612	0.618	0.575	0.575
y	0.382	0.382	0.425	0.406

8. Intensity of Lights

(a) The minimum luminous intensity of lights shall be calculated by using the formula:

$$I = 3.43 \times 10^6 \times T \times D^2 \times K^{-D}$$

where I is luminous intensity in candelas under service conditions,

T is threshold factor 2×10^{-7} lux,

D is range of visibility (luminous range) of the lights in nautical miles,

K is atmospheric transmissivity. For prescribed lights the value of K shall be 0.8, corresponding to a meteorological visibility of approximately 13 nautical miles.

(b) A selection of figures derived from the formula is given in the following table:

Range of visibility (luminous range) of light in nautical miles	Luminous intensity of light in candelas for K = 0.8
D	I
1	0.9
2	4.3
3	12
4	27
5	52
6	94

Note: The maximum luminous intensity of navigation lights should be limited to avoid undue glare. This shall not be achieved by a variable control of the luminous intensity.

The boundaries of the area for each color are given by indicating the corner coordinates, which are as follows:

(1) White:

x	0.525	0.525	0.452	0.310	0.310	0.443
y	0.382	0.440	0.440	0.348	0.283	0.382

(2) Green:

x	0.028	0.009	0.300	0.203
y	0.385	0.723	0.511	0.356

(3) Red:

x	0.680	0.660	0.735	0.721
y	0.320	0.320	0.265	0.259

(4) Yellow:

x	0.612	0.618	0.575	0.575
y	0.382	0.382	0.425	0.406

§ 84.15   Intensity of Lights

(a) The minimum luminous intensity of lights shall be calculated by using the formula:

$$I = 3.43 \times 10^6 \times T \times D^2 \times K^{-D}$$

where I is luminous intensity in candelas under service conditions,

T is threshold factor 2×10^{-7} lux,

D is range of visibility (luminous range) of the lights in nautical miles,

K is atmospheric transmissivity. For prescribed lights the value of K shall be 0.8, corresponding to a meteorological visibility of approximately 13 nautical miles.

(b) A selection of figures derived from the formula is given in Table 84.15 (b).

Table 84.15 (b)

Range of visibility (luminous range) of light in nautical miles	Minimum luminous intensity of light in candelas for K = 0.8
D	I
1	0.9
2	4.3
3	12
4	27
5	52
6	94

9. Horizontal sectors

(a) *(i)* In the forward direction, sidelights as fitted on the vessel shall show the minimum required intensities. The intensities shall decrease to reach practical cut-off between 1 degree and 3 degrees outside the prescribed sectors.

(ii) For sternlights and masthead lights and at 22.5 degrees abaft the beam for sidelights, the minimum required intensities shall be maintained over the arc of the horizon up to 5 degrees within the limits of the sectors prescribed in Rule 21. From 5 degrees within the prescribed sectors the intensity may decrease by 50 percent up to the prescribed limits; it shall decrease steadily to reach practical cut-off at not more than 5 degrees outside the prescribed sectors.

(b) All-round lights shall be so located as not to be obscured by masts, topmasts or structures within angular sectors of more than 6 degrees, except anchor lights prescribed in Rule 30, which need not be placed at an impracticable height above the hull.

10. Vertical sectors

(a) The vertical sectors of electric lights as fitted, with the exception of lights on sailing vessels underway shall ensure that:

(i) at least the required minimum intensity is maintained at all angles from 5 degrees above to 5 degrees below the horizontal;

(ii) at least 60 percent of the required minimum intensity is maintained from 7.5 degrees above to 7.5 degrees below the horizontal.

(b) In the case of sailing vessels underway the vertical sectors of electric lights as fitted shall ensure that:

(i) at least the required minimum intensity is maintained at all angles from 5 degrees above to 5 degrees below the horizontal;

(ii) at least 50 percent of the required minimum intensity is maintained from 25 degrees above to 25 degrees below the horizontal.

(c) In the case of lights other than electric these specifications shall be met as closely as possible.

§ 84.17   Horizontal sectors

(a) (1) In the forward direction, sidelights as fitted on the vessel shall show the minimum required intensities. The intensities shall decrease to reach practical cut-off between 1 and 3 degrees outside the prescribed sectors.

(2) For sternlights and masthead lights and at 22.5 degrees abaft the beam for sidelights, the minimum required intensities shall be maintained over the arc of the horizon up to 5 degrees within the limits of the sectors prescribed in Rule 21. From 5 degrees within the prescribed sectors the intensity may decrease by 50 percent up to the prescribed limits; it shall decrease steadily to reach practical cut-off at not more than 5 degrees outside the prescribed sectors.

(b) All-round lights shall be so located as not to be obscured by masts, topmasts or structures within angular sectors of more than 6 degrees, except anchor lights prescribed in Rule 30, which need not be placed at an impracticable height above the hull, and the all-round white light described in Rule 23 (d), which may not be obscured at all.

§ 84.19   Vertical sectors

(a) The vertical sectors of electric lights as fitted, with the exception of lights on sailing vessels underway and on unmanned barges, shall ensure that:

(1) At least the required minimum intensity is maintained at all angles from 5 degrees above to 5 degrees below the horizontal;

(2) At least 60 percent of the required minimum intensity is maintained from 7.5 degrees above to 7.5 degrees below the horizontal.

(b) In the case of sailing vessels underway the vertical sectors of electric lights as fitted shall ensure that:

(1) At least the required minimum intensity is maintained at all angles from 5 degrees above to 5 degrees below the horizontal;

(2) At least 50 percent of the required minimum intensity is maintained from 25 degrees above to 25 degrees below the horizontal.

(c) In the case of unmanned barges the minimum required intensity of electric lights as fitted shall be maintained on the horizontal.

(d) In the case of lights other than electric lights these specifications shall be met as closely as possible.

11. Intensity of non-electric lights

Non-electric lights shall so far as practicable comply with the minimum intensities, as specified in the Table given in Section 8 of this Annex.

12. Maneuvering light

Notwithstanding the provisions of paragraph 2 (f) of this Annex the maneuvering light described in Rule 34 (b) shall be placed in the same fore and aft vertical plane as the masthead light or lights and, where practicable, at a minimum height of 2 meters vertically above the forward masthead light, provided that it shall be carried not less than 2 meters vertically above or below the after masthead light. On a vessel where only one masthead light is carried the maneuvering light, if fitted, shall be carried where it can best be seen, not less than 2 meters vertically apart from the masthead light.

13. Approval

The construction of lanterns and shapes and the installation of lights on board the vessel shall be to the satisfaction of the appropriate authority of the State whose flag the vessel is entitled to fly.

§ 84.21   Intensity of non-electric lights

Non-electric lights shall so far as practicable comply with the minimum intensities, as specified in the Table given in § 84.15.

§ 84.23   Maneuvering light

Notwithstanding the provisions of § 84.03 (f), the maneuvering light described in Rule 34 (b) shall be placed approximately in the same fore and aft vertical plane as the masthead light or lights and, where practicable, at a minimum height of one-half meter vertically above the forward masthead light, provided that it shall be carried not less than one-half meter vertically above or below the after masthead light. On a vessel where only one masthead light is carried the maneuvering light, if fitted, shall be carried where it can best be seen, not less than one-half meter vertically apart from the masthead light.

§ 84.25   Approval. [Reserved]

ANNEX II: ADDITIONAL SIGNALS FOR FISHING VESSELS FISHING IN CLOSE PROXIMITY

1. General

The lights mentioned herein shall, if exhibited in pursuance of Rule 26 (d), be placed where they can best be seen. They shall be at least 0.9 meter apart but at a lower level than lights prescribed in Rule 26 (b) *(i)* and (c) *(i)*. The lights shall be visible all around the horizon at a distance of at least 1 mile but at a lesser distance from the lights prescribed by these Rules for fishing vessels.

2. Signals for trawlers

(a) Vessels when engaged in trawling, whether using demersal or pelagic gear, may exhibit:
   (i) when shooting their nets: two white lights in a vertical line;
   (ii) when hauling their nets: one white light over one red light in a vertical line;
   (iii) when the net has come fast upon an obstruction: two red lights in a vertical line.

(b) Each vessel engaged in pair trawling may exhibit:
   (i) by night, a searchlight directed forward and in the direction of the other vessel of the pair;
   (ii) when shooting or hauling their nets or when their nets have come fast upon an obstruction, the lights prescribed in 2 (a) above.

3. Signals for purse seiners

Vessels engaged in fishing with purse seine gear may exhibit two yellow lights in a vertical line. These lights shall flash alternately every second and with equal light and occultation duration. These lights may be exhibited only when the vessel is hampered by its fishing gear.

ANNEX II : ADDITIONAL SIGNALS FOR FISHING VESSELS FISHING IN CLOSE PROXIMITY

§ 85.1   General

The lights mentioned herein shall, if exhibited in pursuance of Rule 26 (d), be placed where they can best be seen. They shall be at least 0.9 meter apart but at a lower level than lights prescribed in Rule 26 (b) *(i)* and (c) *(i)* contained in the Inland Navigational Rules Act of 1980. The lights shall be visible all around the horizon at a distance of at least 1 mile but at a lesser distance from the lights prescribed by these Rules for fishing vessels.

§ 85.3   Signals for trawlers

(a) Vessels when engaged in trawling, whether using demersal or pelagic gear, may exhibit:

(1) When shooting their nets: two white lights in a vertical line;

(2) When hauling their nets: one white light over one red light in a vertical line;

(3) When the net has come fast upon an obstruction: two red lights in a vertical line.

(b) Each vessel engaged in pair trawling may exhibit:

(1) By night, a searchlight directed forward and in the direction of the other vessel of the pair;

(2) When shooting or hauling their nets or when their nets have come fast upon an obstruction, the lights prescribed in (a) above.

§ 85.5   Signals for purse seiners

Vessels engaged in fishing with purse seine gear may exhibit two yellow lights in a vertical line. These lights shall flash alternately every second and with equal light and occultation duration. These lights may be exhibited only when the vessel is hampered by its fishing gear.

ANNEX III: TECHNICAL DETAILS OF SOUND SIGNAL APPLIANCES

1. Whistles

(a) Frequencies and range of audibility. The fundamental frequency of the signal shall lie within the range 70-700 Hz.

The range of audibility of the signal from a whistle shall be determined by those frequencies, which may include the fundamental and/or one or more higher frequencies, which lie within the range 180-700 Hz (±1 percent) and which provide the sound pressure levels specified in paragraph 1 (c) below.

(b) Limits of fundamental frequencies. To ensure a wide variety of whistle characteristics, the fundamental frequency of a whistle shall be between the following limits:

(i) 70-200 Hz, for a vessel 200 meters or more in length;

(ii) 130-350 Hz, for a vessel 75 meters but less than 200 meters in length;

(iii) 250-700 Hz, for a vessel less than 75 meters in length.

(c) Sound signal intensity and range of audibility. A whistle fitted in a vessel shall provide, in the direction of maximum intensity of the whistle and at a distance of 1 meter from it, a sound pressure level in at least one 1/3-octave band within the range of frequencies 180-700 Hz (±1 percent) of not less than the appropriate figure given in the table below.

ANNEX III: TECHNICAL DETAILS OF SOUND SIGNAL APPLIANCES

SUBPART A—WHISTLES

§ 86.01   Frequencies and range of audibility.

The fundamental frequency of the signal shall lie within the range 70-525 Hz. The range of audibility of the signal from a whistle shall be determined by those frequencies, which may include the fundamental and/or one or more higher frequencies, which lie within the frequency ranges and provide the sound pressure levels specified in § 86.05.

§ 86.03   Limits of fundamental frequencies.

To ensure a wide variety of whistle characteristics, the fundamental frequency of a whistle shall be between the following limits:

(a) 70-200 Hz, for a vessel 200 meters or more in length;

(b) 130-350 Hz, for a vessel 75 meters but less than 200 meters in length;

(c) 250-525 Hz, for a vessel less than 75 meters in length.

§ 86.05   Sound signal intensity and range of audibility.

A whistle on a vessel shall provide, in the direction of the forward axis of the whistle and at a distance of 1 meter from it, a sound pressure level in at least one 1/3-octave band of not less than the appropriate figure given in Table 86.05 within the following frequency ranges (±1 percent).

Length of vessel in meters	⅓-octave band level at 1 meter in dB referred to $2 \times 10^{-5} \, N/m^2$	Audibility range in nautical miles
200 or more	143	2
75 but less than 200	138	1.5
20 but less than 75	130	1
Less than 20	120	0.5

The range of audibility in the table above is for information and is approximately the range at which a whistle may be heard on its forward axis with 90 percent probability in conditions of still air on board a vessel having average background noise level at the listening posts (taken to be 68 dB in the octave band centered on 250 Hz and 63 dB in the octave band centered on 500 Hz).

In practice the range at which a whistle may be heard is extremely variable and depends critically on weather conditions; the values given can be regarded as typical but under conditions of strong wind or high ambient noise level at the listening post the range may be much reduced.

(d) Directional properties. The sound pressure level of a directional whistle shall be not more than 4 dB below the prescribed sound pressure level on the axis at any direction in the horizontal plane within ±45 degrees of the axis. The sound pressure level at any other direction in the horizontal plane shall be not more than 10 dB below the prescribed sound pressure level on the axis, so that the range in any direction will be at least half the range on the forward axis. The sound pressure level shall be measured in that one-third octave band which determines the audibility range.

Table 86.05

Length of vessel in meters	Fundamental frequency range (Hz)	For measured frequencies (Hz)	⅓-octave band level at 1 meter in dB referred to 2×10^{-5} N/m^2	Audibility range in nautical miles
200 or more	70-200	130-180	145	2
		180-250	143	
		250-1200	140	
75 but less than 200	130-350	130-180	140	1.5
		180-250	138	
		250-1200	134	
20 but less than 75	250-525	250-450	130	1.0
		450-800	125	
		800-1600	121	
12 but less than 20	250-525	250-450	130	0.5
		450-800	115	
		800-2100	111	

Note: The range of audibility in the table above is for information and is approximately the range at which a whistle may usually be heard on its forward axis in conditions of still air on board a vessel having average background noise level at the listening posts (taken to be 68 dB in the octave band centered on 250 Hz and 63 dB in the octave band centered on 500 Hz).

In practice the range at which a whistle may be heard is extremely variable and depends critically on weather conditions; the values given can be regarded as typical but under conditions of strong wind or high ambient noise level at the listening post the range may be much reduced.

§ 86.07   Directional properties.

The sound pressure level of a directional whistle shall be not more than 4 dB below the sound pressure level specified in § 86.05 in any direction in the horizontal plane within ±45 degrees of the forward axis. The sound pressure level of the whistle at any other direction in the horizontal plane shall be not more than 10 dB less than the sound pressure level specified for the forward axis, so that the range of audibility in any direction will be at least half the range required on the forward axis. The sound pressure level shall be measured in that one-third octave band which determines the audibility range.

(e) Positioning of whistles. When a directional whistle is to be used as the only whistle on a vessel, it shall be installed with its maximum intensity directed straight ahead.

A whistle shall be placed as high as practicable on a vessel, in order to reduce interception of the emitted sound by obstructions and also to minimize hearing damage risk to personnel. The sound pressure level of the vessel's own signal at listening posts shall not exceed 110 dB (A) and so far as practicable should not exceed 100 dB (A).

(f) Fitting of more than one whistle. If whistles are fitted at a distance apart of more than 100 meters, it shall be so arranged that they are not sounded simultaneously.

(g) Combined whistle systems. If due to the presence of obstructions the sound field of a single whistle or of one of the whistles referred to in paragraph 1 (f) above is likely to have a zone of greatly reduced signal level, it is recommended that a combined whistle system be fitted so as to overcome this reduction. For the purposes of the Rules a combined whistle system is to be regarded as a single whistle. The whistles of a combined system shall be located at a distance apart of not more than 100 meters and arranged to be sounded simultaneously. The frequency of any one whistle shall differ from those of the others by at least 10 Hz.

§ 86.09   Positioning of whistles.

(a) When a directional whistle is to be used as the only whistle on the vessel and is permanently installed, it shall be installed with its forward axis directed forward.

(b) A whistle shall be placed as high as practicable on a vessel, in order to reduce interception of the emitted sound by obstructions and also to minimize hearing damage risk to personnel. The sound pressure level of the vessel's own signal at listening posts shall not exceed 110 dB (A) and so far as practicable should not exceed 100 dB (A).

§ 86.11   Fitting of more than one whistle.

If whistles are fitted at a distance apart of more than 100 meters, they shall not be sounded simultaneously.

§ 86.13   Combined whistle systems.

(a) A combined whistle system is a number of whistles (sound emitting sources) operated together. For the purposes of the Rules a combined whistle system is to be regarded as a single whistle.

(b) The whistles of a combined system shall—

(1) Be located at a distance apart of not more than 100 meters,

(2) Be sounded simultaneously,

(3) Each have a fundamental frequency different from those of the others by at least 10 Hz, and

(4) Have a tonal characteristic appropriate for the length of vessel which shall be evidenced by at least two-thirds of the whistles in the combined system having fundamental frequencies falling within the limits prescribed in § 86.03, or if there are only two whistles in the combined system, by the higher fundamental frequency falling within the limits prescribed in § 86.03.

> Note: If due to the presence of obstructions the sound field of a single whistle or of one of the whistles referred to in § 86.11 is likely to have a zone of greatly reduced signal level, a combined whistle system should be fitted so as to overcome this reduction.

§ 86.15   Towing vessel whistles.

A power-driven vessel normally engaged in pushing ahead or towing alongside may, at all times, use a whistle whose characteristic falls within the limits prescribed by § 86.03 for the longest customary composite length of the vessel and its tow.

2. Bell or gong

(a) Intensity of signal. A bell or gong, or other device having similar sound characteristics shall produce a sound pressure level of not less than 110 dB at a distance of 1 meter from it.

(b) Construction. Bells and gongs shall be made of corrosion-resistant material and designed to give a clear tone. The diameter of the mouth of the bell shall be not less than 300 mm for vessels of 20 meters or more in length, and shall be not less than 200 mm for vessels of 12 meters or more but of less than 20 meters in length. Where practicable, a power-driven bell striker is recommended to ensure constant force but manual operation shall be possible. The mass of the striker shall be not less than 3 percent of the mass of the bell.

3. Approval

The construction of sound signal appliances, their performance and their installation on board the vessel shall be to the satisfaction of the appropriate authority of the State whose flag the vessel is entitled to fly.

SUBPART B—BELL OR GONG

§ 86.21   Intensity of signal.

A bell or gong, or other device having similar sound characteristics shall produce a sound pressure level of not less than 110 dB at 1 meter.

§ 86.23   Construction.

Bells and gongs shall be made of corrosion-resistant material and designed to give a clear tone. The diameter of the mouth of the bell shall be not less than 300 mm for vessels of more than 20 meters in length, and shall be not less than 200 mm for vessels of 12 to 20 meters in length. The mass of the striker shall be not less than 3 percent of the mass of the bell. The striker shall be capable of manual operation.

Note: When practicable, a power-driven bell striker is recommended to ensure constant force.

SUBPART C—APPROVAL

§ 86.31   Approval. [Reserved]

ANNEX IV: DISTRESS SIGNALS

1. Need of assistance

The following signals, used or exhibited either together or separately, indicate distress and need of assistance:

(a) a gun or other explosive signal fired at intervals of about a minute;

(b) a continuous sounding with any fog-signalling apparatus;

(c) rockets or shells, throwing red stars fired one at a time at short intervals;

(d) a signal made by radiotelegraphy or by any other signalling method consisting of the group . . . — — — . . . (SOS) in the Morse Code;

(e) a signal sent by radiotelephony consisting of the spoken word "Mayday";

(f) the International Code Signal of distress indicated by N.C.;

(g) a signal consisting of a square flag having above or below it a ball or anything resembling a ball;

(h) flames on the vessel (as from a burning tar barrel, oil barrel, etc);

(i) a rocket parachute flare or a hand flare showing a red light;

(j) a smoke signal giving off orange-colored smoke;

(k) slowly and repeatedly raising and lowering arms outstretched to each side;

(l) the radiotelegraph alarm signal;

(m) the radiotelephone alarm signal;

(n) signals transmitted by emergency position-indicating radio beacons.

(o) approved signals transmitted by radiocommunication systems.

ANNEX IV: DISTRESS SIGNALS

§ 87.1   Need of assistance

The following signals, used or exhibited either together or separately, indicate distress and need of assistance:

(a) A gun or other explosive signal fired at intervals of about a minute;

(b) A continuous sounding with any fog-signalling apparatus;

(c) Rockets or shells, throwing red stars fired one at a time at short intervals;

(d) A signal made by radiotelegraphy or by any other signalling method consisting of the group . . . — — — . . . (SOS) in the Morse Code;

(e) A signal sent by radiotelephony consisting of the spoken word "Mayday" ;

(f) The International Code Signal of distress indicated by N.C.;

(g) A signal consisting of a square flag having above or below it a ball or anything resembling a ball;

(h) Flames on the vessel (as from a burning tar barrel, oil barrel, etc.);

(i) A rocket parachute flare or a hand flare showing a red light;

(j) A smoke signal giving off orange-colored smoke;

(k) Slowly and repeatedly raising and lowering arms outstretched to each side;

(l) The radiotelegraph alarm signal;

(m) The radiotelephone alarm signal;

(n) Signals transmitted by emergency position-indicating radio beacons;

(o) Signals transmitted by radiocommunication systems;

(p) A high intensity white light flashing at regular intervals from 50 to 70 times per minute.

2. The use or exhibition of any of the foregoing signals except for the purpose of indicating distress and need of assistance and the use of other signals which may be confused with any of the above signals is prohibited.

3. Attention is drawn to the relevant sections of the International Code of Signals, the Merchant Ship Search and Rescue Manual and the following signals:

(a) a piece of orange-colored canvas with either a black square and circle or other appropriate symbol (for identification from the air);
(b) a dye marker.

§ 87.3   Exclusive use.

The use or exhibition of any of the foregoing signals except for the purpose of indicating distress and need of assistance and the use of other signals which may be confused with any of the above signals is prohibited.

§ 87.5   Supplemental signals.

Attention is drawn to the relevant sections of the International Code of Signals, the Merchant Ship Search and Rescue Manual, the International Telecommunication Union Radio Regulations, and the following signals:

(a) A piece of orange-colored canvas with either a black square and circle or other appropriate symbol (for identification from the air);

(b) A dye marker.

ANNEX V: PILOT RULES

§ 88.01   Purpose and applicability.

This Part applies to all vessels operating on United States inland waters and to United States vessels operating on the Canadian waters of the Great Lakes to the extent there is no conflict with Canadian law.

§ 88.03   Definitions.

The terms used in this part have the same meaning as defined in the Inland Navigational Rules Act of 1980.

§ 88.05   Copy of Rules.

After January 1, 1983, the operator of each self-propelled vessel 12 meters or more in length shall carry on board and maintain for ready reference a copy of the Inland Navigation Rules.

§ 88.09   Temporary exemption from light and shape requirements when operating under bridges.

A vessel's navigation lights and shapes may be lowered if necessary to pass under a bridge.

§ 88.11   Law enforcement vessels.

(a) Law enforcement vessels may display a flashing blue light when engaged in direct law enforcement activities. This light shall be located so that it does not interfere with the visibility of the vessel's navigation lights.

(b) The blue light described in this section may be displayed by law enforcement vessels of the United States and the States and their political subdivisions.

§ 88.13   Lights on barges at bank or dock.

(a) The following barges shall display at night and, if practicable, in periods of restricted visibility the lights described in paragraph (b) of this section—

(1) Every barge projecting into a buoyed or restricted channel.

(2) Every barge so moored that it reduces the available navigable width of any channel to less than 80 meters.

(3) Barges moored in groups more than two barges wide or to a maximum width of over 25 meters.

(4) Every barge not moored parallel to the bank or dock.

(b) Barges described in paragraph (a) shall carry two unobstructed white lights of an intensity to be visible for at least one mile on a clear dark night, and arranged as follows:

(1) On a single moored barge, lights shall be placed on the two corners farthest from the bank or dock.

(2) On barges moored in group formation, a light shall be placed on each of the upstream and downstream ends of the group, on the corners farthest from the bank or dock.

(3) Any barge in a group, projecting from the main body of the group toward the channel, shall be lighted as a single barge.

(c) Barges moored in any slip or slough which is used primarily for mooring purposes are exempt from the lighting requirements of this section.

(d) Barges moored in well-illuminated areas are exempt from the lighting requirements of this section. These areas are as follows:

Chicago Sanitary Ship Canal
(1) Mile 293.2 to 293.9
(3) Mile 295.2 to 296.1
(5) Mile 297.5 to 297.8
(7) Mile 298 to 298.2
(9) Mile 298.6 to 298.8
(11) Mile 299.3 to 299.4
(13) Mile 299.8 to 300.5
(15) Mile 303 to 303.2
(17) Mile 303.7 to 303.9
(19) Mile 305.7 to 305.8
(21) Mile 310.7 to 310.9
(23) Mile 311 to 311.2
(25) Mile 312.5 to 312.6
(27) Mile 313.8 to 314.2
(29) Mile 314.6
(31) Mile 314.8 to 315.3
(33) Mile 315.7 to 316
(35) Mile 316.8
(37) Mile 316.85 to 317.05
(39) Mile 317.5
(41) Mile 318.4 to 318.9

(43) Mile 318.7 to 318.8
(45) Mile 320 to 320.3
(47) Mile 320.6
(49) Mile 322.3 to 322.4
(51) Mile 322.8
(53) Mile 322.9 to 327.2
Calumet Sag Channel
(61) Mile 316.5
Little Calumet River
(71) Mile 321.2
(73) Mile 322.3
Calumet River
(81) Mile 328.5 to 328.7
(83) Mile 329.2 to 329.4
(85) Mile 330, west bank to 330.2
(87) Mile 331.4 to 331.6
(89) Mile 332.2 to 332.4
(91) Mile 332.6 to 332.8
Cumberland River
(101) Mile 126.8
(103) Mile 191

§ 88.15   Lights on dredge pipelines.

Dredge pipelines that are floating or supported on trestles shall display the following lights at night and in periods of restricted visibility.

(a) One row of yellow lights. The lights must be—

(1) Flashing 50 to 70 times per minute,

(2) Visible all around the horizon,

(3) Visible for at least 2 miles on a clear dark night,

(4) Not less than 1 and not more than 3.5 meters above the water,

(5) Approximately equally spaced, and

(6) Not more than 10 meters apart where the pipeline crosses a navigable channel. Where the pipeline does not cross a navigable channel the lights must be sufficient in number to clearly show the pipeline's length and course.

(b) Two red lights at each end of the pipeline, including the ends in a channel where the pipeline is separated to allow vessels to pass (whether open or closed). The lights must be—

(1) Visible all around the horizon, and

(2) Visible for at least 2 miles on a clear dark night, and

(3) One meter apart in a vertical line with the lower light at the same height above the water as the flashing yellow light.

RELATED GOVERNMENT REGULATIONS

PENALTY PROVISIONS

Violations of International Navigation Rules and Regulations (33 U.S.C. 1608)

Sec. 9.(a) Whoever operates a vessel, subject to the provisions of this Act, in violation of this Act or of any regulation promulgated pursuant to section 8, shall be liable to a civil penalty of not more than $5,000 for each such violation.

(b) Every vessel subject to the provisions of this Act, other than a public vessel being used for noncommercial purposes, which is operated in violation of this Act or of any regulation promulgated pursuant to section 8, shall be liable to a civil penalty of not more than $5,000 for each such violation, for which penalty the vessel may be seized and proceeded against in the district court of the United States of any district within which such vessel may be found.

(c) The Secretary of the department in which the Coast Guard is operating may assess any civil penalty authorized by this section. No such penalty may be assessed until the person charged, or the owner of the vessel charged, as appropriate, shall have been given notice of the violation involved and an opportunity for a hearing. For good cause shown, the Secretary may remit, mitigate, or compromise any penalty assessed. Upon the failure of the person charged, or the owner of the vessel charged, to pay an assessed penalty, as it may have been mitigated or compromised, the Secretary may request the Attorney General to commence an action in the appropriate district court of the United States for collection of the penalty as assessed, without regard to the amount involved, together with such other relief as may be appropriate. (July 27, 1977, § 9, 91 Stat. 310)

Violations of Inland Navigation Rules and Regulations (33 U.S.C. 2072)

Sec. 4.(a) Whoever operates a vessel in violation of this Act, or of any regulation issued thereunder, or in violation of a certificate of alternative compliance issued under Rule 1 is liable to a civil penalty of not more than $5,000 for each violation.

(b) Every vessel subject to this Act, other than a public vessel being used for noncommercial purposes, that is operated in violation of this Act, or of any regulation issued thereunder, or in violation of a certificate of alternative compliance issued under Rule 1 is liable to a civil penalty of not more than $5,000 for each violation, for which penalty the vessel may be seized and proceeded against in the district court of the United States of any district within which the vessel may be found.

(c) The Secretary may assess any civil penalty authorized by this section. No such penalty may be assessed until the person charged, or the owner of the vessel charged, as appropriate, shall have been given notice of the violation involved and an opportunity for a hearing. For good cause shown, the Secretary may remit, mitigate, or compromise any penalty assessed. Upon the failure of the person charged, or the owner of the vessel charged, to pay an assessed penalty, as it may have been mitigated or compromised, the Secretary may request the Attorney General to commence an action in the appropriate district court of the United States for collection of the penalty as assessed, without regard to the amount involved, together with such other relief as may be appropriate.

(d) The Secretary of the Treasury shall withhold or revoke, at the request of the Secretary, the clearance, required by section 4197 of the Revised Statutes of the United States (46 U.S.C. 91) of any vessel, the owner or operator of which is subject to any of the penalties in this section. Clearance may be granted in such cases upon the filing of a bond or other surety satisfactory to the Secretary. (Dec. 24, 1980, § 4, 94 Stat. 3433)

Penalties for Negligent Operations; Duties Related to Marine Casualty Assistance and Information; Duty to Provide Assistance at Sea; Injunctions (46 U.S.C. 2301-2305)

Excerpt from Title 46 of the United States Code

Chapter 23—Operations of Vessels Generally [Enacted on August 26, 1983]

§ 2301   Application.

This chapter applies to a vessel operated on waters subject to the jurisdiction of the United States and, for a vessel owned in the United States, on the high seas.

§ 2302   Penalties for negligent operations.

(a) A person operating a vessel in a negligent manner that endangers the life, limb, or property of a person is liable to the United States Government for a civil penalty of not more than $1,000.

(b) A person operating a vessel in a grossly negligent manner that endangers the life, limb, or property of a person shall be fined not more than $5,000, imprisoned for not more than one year, or both.

(c) For a penalty imposed under this section, the vessel also is liable in rem unless the vessel is—

(1) owned by a State or a political subdivision of a State;

(2) operated principally for governmental purposes; and

(3) identified clearly as a vessel of that State or subdivision.

§ 2303   Duties related to marine casualty assistance and information.

(a) The master or individual in charge of a vessel involved in a marine casualty shall—

(1) render necessary assistance to each individual affected to save that affected individual from danger caused by the marine casualty, so far as the master or individual in charge can do so without

serious danger to the master's or individual's vessel or to individuals on board; and

(2) give the master's or individual's name and address and identification of the vessel to the master or individual in charge of any other vessel involved in the casualty, to any individual injured, and to the owner of any property damaged.

(b) An individual violating this section or a regulation prescribed under this section shall be fined not more than $1,000 or imprisoned for not more than 2 years. The vessel also is liable in rem to the United States Government for the fine.

(c) An individual complying with subsection (a) of this section or gratuitously and in good faith rendering assistance at the scene of a marine casualty without objection by an individual assisted, is not liable for damages as a result of rendering assistance or for an act or omission in providing or arranging salvage, towage, medical treatment, or other assistance when the individual acts as an ordinary, reasonable, and prudent individual would have acted under the circumstances.

§ 2304   Duty to provide assistance at sea.

(a) A master or individual in charge of a vessel shall render assistance to any individual found at sea in danger of being lost, so far as the master or individual in charge can do so without serious danger to the master's or individual's vessel or individuals on board.

(b) A master or individual violating this section shall be fined not more than $1,000, imprisoned for not more than 2 years, or both.

§ 2305   Injunctions.

(a) The district courts of the United States have jurisdiction to enjoin the negligent operation of vessels prohibited by this chapter on the petition of the Attorney General for the United States Government.

(b) When practicable, the Secretary shall—

(1) give notice to any person against whom an action for injunctive relief is considered under this section an opportunity to present that person's views; and

(2) except for a knowing and willful violation, give the person a reasonable opportunity to achieve compliance.

(c) The failure to give notice and opportunity to present views under subsection (b) of this section does not preclude the court from granting appropriate relief.

DISTINCTIVE LIGHTS AUTHORIZED FOR SUBMARINES

The Secretary of the Navy has authorized the display of a distinctive light by U. S. Naval submarines to be used when operating under either the International Rules or the Inland Rules (Part 707 of Title 32, Code of Federal Regulations). This light is exhibited in addition to the normal navigation lights.

Submarines with normal navigation lights may easily be mistaken for small vessels. Since submarines are large deep draft vessels with limited maneuvering characteristics while they are on the surface, it is necessary to provide them with an additional unique identification light.

U. S. submarines may therefore display an intermittent flashing amber beacon with a sequence of operation of one flash per second for three (3) seconds followed by a three (3) second off-period. The light will be located where it can best be seen, as near as practicable, all around the horizon. It shall not be located less than two (2) feet above or below the masthead lights.

ALTERNATIVE COMPLIANCE

The alternative compliance procedures for the International Rules and the Inland Rules are the same, although they appear both in the International Rules section of the Code of Federal Regulations (33 CFR Part 81) and in the Inland Rules section (33 CFR Part 89).

Sec.
1. Definitions.
2. General.
3. Application for a certificate of alternative compliance.
4. Certificate of alternative compliance: Contents.
5. Certificate of alternative compliance: Termination.
6. Record of certification of vessels of special construction or purpose.

1. Definitions.

As used in this part:
"72 COLREGS" refers to the International Regulations for Preventing Collisions at Sea, 1972, done at London, October 20, 1972, as rectified by the Proces-Verbal of December 1, 1973, as amended.

"Inland Rules" refers to the Inland Navigation Rules contained in the Inland Navigational Rules Act of 1980 (Pub. L. 96-591) and the technical annexes established under that act.

"A vessel of special construction or purpose" means a vessel designed or modified to perform a special function and whose arrangement is thereby made relatively inflexible.

"Interference with the special function of the vessel" occurs when installation or use of lights, shapes, or sound-signaling appliances under the 72 COLREGS/Inland Rules prevents or significantly hinders the operation in which the vessel is usually engaged.

2. General.

Vessels of special construction or purpose which cannot fully comply with the light, shape, and sound signal provisions of the 72 COLREGS/Inland Rules without interfering with their special function may instead meet alternative requirements. The Chief of the Marine Safety Division in each Coast Guard District Office makes this determination and requires that alternative compliance be as close as possible with the 72 COLREGS/Inland Rules. These regulations set out the procedure by which a vessel may be certified for alternative compliance.

3. Application for a Certificate of Alternative Compliance.

(a) The owner, builder, operator, or agent of a vessel of special construction or purpose who believes the vessel cannot fully comply with the 72 COLREGS/Inland Rules light, shape, or sound signal provisions without interference with its special function may apply for a determination that alternative compliance is justified. The application must be in writing, submitted to the Chief of the Marine Safety Division of the Coast Guard District in which the vessel is being built or operated, and include the following information:

(1) The name, address, and telephone number of the applicant.
(2) The identification of the vessel by its—
(i) Official number;
(ii) Shipyard hull number;
(iii) Hull identification number; or
(iv) State number, if the vessel does not have an official number or hull identification number.
(3) Vessel name and home port, if known.
(4) A description of the vessel's area of operation.

(5) A description of the provision for which the Certificate of Alternative Compliance is sought, including:

(i) The 72 COLREGS/Inland Rules Rule or Annex section number for which the Certificate of Alternative Compliance is sought;

(ii) A description of the special function of the vessel that would be interfered with by full compliance with the provision of that Rule or Annex section; and

(iii) A statement of how full compliance would interfere with the special function of the vessel.

(6) A description of the alternative installation that is in closest possible compliance with the applicable 72 COLREGS/Inland Rules Rule or Annex section.

(7) A copy of the vessel's plans or an accurate scale drawing that clearly shows—

(i) The required installation of the equipment under the 72 COLREGS/Inland Rules,

(ii) The proposed installation of the equipment for which certification is being sought, and

(iii) Any obstructions that may interfere with the equipment when installed in—

(A) The required location; and

(B) The proposed location.

(b) The Coast Guard may request from the applicant additional information concerning the application.

4. Certificate of Alternative Compliance: Contents.

The Chief of the Marine Safety Division issues the Certificate of Alternative Compliance to the vessel based on a determination that it cannot comply fully with 72 COLREGS/Inland Rules light, shape, and sound signal provisions without interference with its special function. This Certificate includes—

(a) Identification of the vessel as supplied in the application;

(b) The provision of the 72 COLREGS/Inland Rules for which the Certificate authorizes alternative compliance;

(c) A certification that the vessel is unable to comply fully with the 72 COLREGS/Inland Rules light, shape, and sound signal requirements without interference with its special function;

(d) A statement of why full compliance would interfere with the special function of the vessel;

(e) The required alternative installation;

(f) A statement that the required alternative installation is in the closest possible compliance with the 72 COLREGS/Inland Rules without interfering with the special function of the vessel;

(g) The date of issuance;

(h) A statement that the Certificate of Alternative Compliance terminates when the vessel ceases to be usually engaged in the operation for which the certificate is issued.

5. Certificate of Alternative Compliance: Termination.

The Certificate of Alternative Compliance terminates if the information supplied under 3.(a) or the Certificate issued under 4. is no longer applicable to the vessel.

6. Record of Certification of Vessels of Special Construction or Purpose.

(a) Copies of Certificates of Alternative Compliance and documentation concerning Coast Guard vessels are available for inspection at Coast Guard Headquarters, Office of Navigation, 2100 Second Street S.W., Washington, D.C. 20593.

(b) The owner or operator of a vessel issued a Certificate shall ensure that the vessel does not operate unless the Certificate of Alternative Compliance or a certified copy of that Certificate is on board the vessel and available for inspection by Coast Guard personnel.

Vessel Bridge-to-Bridge Radiotelephone Regulations (33 CFR 26)

Sec.

26.01 Purpose.	26.06 Maintenance of radiotele-
26.02 Definitions.	phone; failure of radiotelephone.
26.03 Radiotelephone required.	26.07 English language.
26.04 Use of the designated	26.08 Exemption procedures.
frequency.	26.09 List of exemptions.
26.05 Use of radiotelephone.	26.10 Penalties.

Authority: 85 Stat. 164; 33 U.S.C. 1201-1208; 49 CFR 1.46 (o) (2), unless otherwise noted.

Source: CGD 71-114R, 37 FR 12720, June 28, 1972, unless otherwise noted.

§ 26.01   Purpose.

(a) The purpose of this part is to implement the provisions of the Vessel Bridge-to-Bridge Radiotelephone Act. This part—

(1) Requires the use of the vessel bridge-to-bridge radiotelephone;

(2) Provides the Coast Guard's interpretation of the meaning of important terms in the Act;

(3) Prescribes the procedures for applying for an exemption from the Act and the regulations issued under the Act and a listing of exemptions.

(b) Nothing in this part relieves any person from the obligation of complying with the rules of the road and the applicable pilot rules.

§ 26.02   Definitions.

For the purpose of this part and interpreting the Act—

"Secretary" means the Secretary of the Department in which the Coast Guard is operating;

"Act" means the "Vessel Bridge-to-Bridge Radiotelephone Act", 33 U.S.C. sections 1201-1208;

"Length" is measured from end to end over the deck excluding sheer;

"Power-driven vessel" means any vessel propelled by machinery; and

"Towing vessel" means any commercial vessel engaged in towing another vessel astern, alongside, or by pushing ahead.

(Rule 1, International Regulations for Preventing Collisions at Sea, 1972 (as rectified); EO 11964 (14 U.S.C. 2); 49 CFR 1.46(b))

[CGD 71-114R, 37 FR 12720, June 28,1972, as amended by CGD 77-118a, 42 FR 35784, July 11, 1977]

§ 26.03   Radiotelephone required.

(a) Unless an exemption is granted under § 26.09 and except as provided in paragraph (a) (4) of this section, section 4 of the Act provides that—

(1) Every power-driven vessel of sixty-five feet or more in length while navigating;

(2) Every vessel of 100 gross tons and upward carrying one or more passengers for hire while navigating;

(3) Every towing vessel of 26 feet or over in length while navigating; and

(4) Every dredge and floating plant engaged in or near a channel or fairway in operations likely to restrict or affect navigation of other vessels: *Provided,* That an unmanned or intermittently manned floating plant under the control of a dredge need not be required to have separate radiotelephone capability;

Shall have a radiotelephone capable of operation from its navigational bridge, or in the case of a dredge, from its main control station, and capable of transmitting and receiving on the frequency or frequencies within the 156-162 Mega-Hertz band using the classes of emissions designated by the Federal Communications Commission, after consultation with other cognizant agencies, for the exchange of navigational information.

(b) The radiotelephone required by paragraph (a) of this section shall be carried on board the described vessels, dredges, and floating plants upon the navigable waters of the United States inside the lines established pursuant to section 2 of the Act of February 19, 1895 (28 Stat. 672), as amended.

§ 26.04   Use of the designated frequency.

(a) No person may use the frequency designated by the Federal Communications Commission under section 8 of the Act, 33 U.S.C. 1207 (a), to transmit any information other than information necessary for the safe navigation of vessels or necessary tests.

(b) Each person who is required to maintain a listening watch under section 5 of the Act shall, when necessary, transmit and confirm, on the designated frequency, the intentions of his vessel and any other information necessary for the safe navigation of vessels.

(c) Nothing in these regulations may be construed as prohibiting the use of the designated frequency to communicate with shore stations to obtain or furnish information necessary for the safe navigation of vessels.

Note: The Federal Communications Commission has designated the frequency 156.65 MHz for the use of bridge-to-bridge radiotelephone stations.

§26.05   Use of radiotelephone.

Section 5 of the Act states—

(a) The radiotelephone required by this Act is for the exclusive use of the master or person in charge of the vessel, or the person designated by the master or person in charge to pilot or direct the movement of the vessel, who shall maintain a listening watch on the designated frequency. Nothing contained herein shall be interpreted as precluding the use of portable radiotelephone equipment to satisfy the requirements of this Act.

§ 26.06   Maintenance of radiotelephone; failure of radiotelephone.—

Section 6 of the Act states—

(a) Whenever radiotelephone capability is required by this Act, a vessel's radiotelephone equipment shall be maintained in effective operating condition. If the radiotelephone equipment carried aboard a vessel ceases to operate, the master shall exercise due diligence to restore it or cause it to be restored to effective operating condition at the earliest practicable time. The failure of a vessel's radiotelephone equipment shall not, in itself, constitute a violation of this Act, nor shall it obligate the master of any vessel to moor or anchor his vessel; however, the loss of radiotelephone capability shall be given consideration in the navigation of the vessel.

§ 26.07   English language.

No person may use the services of, and no person may serve as a person required to maintain a listening watch under section 5 of the Act, 33 U.S.C. 1204 unless he can speak the English language.

§ 26.08   Exemption procedures.

(a) Any person may petition for an exemption from any provision of the Act or this part;

(b) Each petition must be submitted in writing to U. S. Coast Guard (G-N), 2100 Second Street, S.W., Washington, D.C. 20593, and must state—

(1) The provisions of the Act or this part from which an exemption is requested; and

(2) The reasons why marine navigation will not be adversely affected if the exemption is granted and if the exemption relates to a local communication system how that system would fully comply with the intent of the concept of the Act but would not conform in detail if the exemption is granted.

[CGD 71-114R, 37 FR 12720, June 28, 1972, as amended by CGD 73-256, 39 FR 9176, Mar. 8, 1974]

§ 26.09   List of exemptions.

(a) All vessels navigating on those waters governed by the navigation rules for the Great Lakes and their connecting and tributary waters (33 U.S.C. 241 et seq.) are exempt from the requirements of the Vessel Bridge-to-Bridge Radiotelephone Act and this part until May 6,1975.

(b) Each vessel navigating on the waters under the navigation rules for the Great Lakes and their connecting and tributary waters (33 U.S.C. 241 et seq.) and to which the Vessel Bridge-to-Bridge Radiotelephone Act (33 U.S.C. 1201-1208) applies is exempt from the requirements in 33 U.S.C. 1203, 1204, and 1205 and the regulations under § 26.03, 26.04, 26.05, 26.06, and 26.07. Each of these vessels and each person to whom 33 U.S.C. 1208(a) applies must comply with Articles VII, X, XI, XII, XIII, XV, and XVI and Technical Regulations 1-7 of "The Agreement Between the United States of America and Canada for Promotion of Safety on the Great Lakes by Means of Radio, 1973".

[CGD 72-223R, 37 FR 28633, Dec. 28, 1972, as amended by CGD 74-291, 39 FR 44980, Dec. 30, 1974; CGD 74-304, 40 FR 19470, May 5, 1975]

§ 26.10   Penalties. Section 9 of the Act states—

(a) Whoever, being the master or person in charge of a vessel subject to the Act, fails to enforce or comply with the Act or the regulations hereunder; or whoever, being designated by the master or person in charge of a vessel subject to the Act to pilot or direct the movement of a vessel fails to enforce or comply with the Act or the regulations hereunder—is liable to a civil penalty of not more than $500 to be assessed by the Secretary.

(b) Every vessel navigated in violation of the Act or the regulations hereunder is liable to a civil penalty of not more than $500 to be assessed by the Secretary, for which the vessel may be proceeded against in any District Court of the United States having jurisdiction.

(c) Any penalty assessed under this section may be remitted or mitigated by the Secretary, upon such terms as he may deem proper.

QUESTIONS ON THE
RULES OF THE ROAD

1. INLAND ONLY. For the purpose of the Inland Navigation Rules, the term "inland waters" includes _____.
   A. the Western Rivers
   B. the Great Lakes on the United States side of the International Boundary
   C. harbors and rivers shoreward of the COLREGS demarcation lines
   D. all of the above
2. INLAND ONLY. Which statement is true concerning the Inland Navigation Rules?
   A. The Rules require vessels to comply with VTS regulations.
   B. The Rules use the term "safe speed."
   C. The Rules provide for action to be taken by a stand-on vessel in a crossing situation prior to being in extremis.
   D. All of the above
3. INLAND ONLY. You are onboard the stand-on vessel in a crossing situation. Upon sounding a one-blast whistle signal the give-way vessel answers with a two-blast whistle signal. You should then sound the danger signal and _____.
   A. maintain course and speed, as you are the stand-on vessel
   B. come around sharply to port
   C. stop and back your vessel if necessary until signals are agreed on
   D. maneuver around the stern of the other vessel
4. INLAND ONLY. In a narrow channel, you are underway on Vessel A and desire to overtake Vessel B. After you sound two short blasts on your whistle, Vessel B sounds five short rapid blasts on the whistle. You should _____.
   A. pass with caution on the port side of Vessel B
   B. hold your relative position, and then initiate another signal after the situation has stabilized
   C. answer the five-short-blast signal then stop your vessel until the other vessel initiates a signal
   D. slow or stop and expect radical maneuvers from Vessel B
5. INLAND ONLY. You are proceeding up a channel in Chesapeake Bay and are meeting an outbound vessel. Your responsibilities include _____.
   A. keeping to that side of the channel which is on your vessel's port side
   B. stopping your vessel and letting the outbound vessel initiate the signals for meeting and passing
   C. appropriately answering any whistle signals given by the other vessel
   D. giving the outbound vessel the right-of-way

6. INLAND ONLY. Your vessel is proceeding down a channel, and can safely navigate only within the channel. Another vessel is crossing your bow from port to starboard, and you are in doubt as to his intentions. Which statement is true?
    A. The sounding of the danger signal is optional.
    B. The sounding of the danger signal is mandatory.
    C. You should sound two short blasts.
    D. You should sound one prolonged and two short blasts.

7. INLAND ONLY. Which is true of a downbound power-driven vessel, when meeting an upbound vessel on the Western Rivers?
    A. She has the right-of-way.
    B. She shall propose the manner of passage.
    C. She shall initiate maneuvering signals.
    D. All of the above

8. INLAND ONLY. Which is true of a downbound vessel, when meeting an upbound vessel on the Western Rivers?
    A. She has the right-of-way only if she is a power-driven vessel.
    B. She has the right-of-way only if she has a tow.
    C. She does not have the right-of-way, since the other vessel is not crossing the river.
    D. She must wait for a whistle signal from the upbound vessel.

9. INLAND ONLY. Your vessel is meeting another vessel head to head. To comply with the steering and sailing rules you should _____.
    A. exchange one short blast, alter course to the left, and pass starboard to starboard
    B. exchange one short blast, alter course to the right, and pass port to port
    C. exchange two short blasts, alter course to the left, and pass starboard to starboard
    D. exchange two short blasts, alter course to the right, and pass port to port

10. INLAND ONLY. A vessel crossing a river on the Great Lakes or Western Rivers must keep out of the way of a power-driven vessel _____.
    A. descending the river with a tow
    B. ascending the river with a tow
    C. ascending the river without a tow
    D. all of the above

11. INLAND ONLY. On the Western Rivers, a vessel crossing a river must _____.
    A. only keep out of the way of a power-driven vessel descending the river
    B. keep out of the way of any vessel descending the river
    C. keep out of the way of a power-driven vessel ascending or descending the river
    D. keep out of the way of any vessel ascending or descending the river

12. INLAND ONLY. If your tug is pushing a barge ahead at night, what light(s) should show aft on your vessel?
    A. A white sternlight
    B. Two red lights
    C. Two towing lights
    D. Three white lights

13. INLAND ONLY. A power-driven vessel when pushing ahead or towing alongside on the Western Rivers shall carry _____.
    A. two masthead lights, sidelights, and a sternlight
    B. two masthead lights, sidelights, and two towing lights
    C. sidelights and two towing lights
    D. one masthead light, sidelights, and a sternlight

14. INLAND ONLY. A special flashing light is used on a vessel _____.
    A. being pushed ahead
    B. towed alongside
    C. towed astern
    D. any of the above

15. INLAND ONLY. A vessel of less than 20 meters at anchor at night in a "special anchorage area" _____.
    A. must show one white light
    B. need not show any lights
    C. must show two white lights
    D. must show a light only on the approach of another vessel

16. INLAND ONLY. What type of light is required if a vessel uses this light to signal passing intentions?
    A. An all-round white light only
    B. An all-round yellow light only
    C. An all-round white or yellow light
    D. Any colored light is acceptable.

17. INLAND ONLY. You are overtaking another vessel in a narrow channel. The other vessel will have to move to allow you to pass. You wish to overtake the other vessel and leave her on your starboard side. Your first whistle signal should be _____.
    A. one short blast
    B. two short blasts
    C. two prolonged blasts followed by one short blast
    D. two prolonged blasts followed by two short blasts

18. INLAND ONLY. You are crossing the course of another vessel which is to your starboard. You have reached an agreement by radiotelephone to pass astern of the other vessel. You must _____.
    A. sound one short blast
    B. sound two short blasts
    C. change course to starboard
    D. none of the above

19. INLAND ONLY. A vessel leaving a dock or berth must sound a prolonged blast of the whistle only if _____.
    A. other vessels can be seen approaching
    B. she is a power-driven vessel
    C. visibility is restricted
    D. her engines are going astern

20. INLAND ONLY. Which of the following light displays would mark the opening in a pipeline where vessels could pass through?
    - A. Three red lights in a vertical line on each side of the opening
    - B. Two red lights in a vertical line on each side of the opening
    - C. Three white lights in a vertical line on each side of the opening
    - D. Two white lights in a vertical line on each side of the opening

21. INLAND ONLY. At night a barge moored in a slip used primarily for mooring purposes shall _____.
    - A. not be required to be lighted
    - B. show a white light at each corner
    - C. show a red light at the bow and stern
    - D. show a flashing yellow light at each corner

22. INLAND ONLY. What light(s) shall be shown at night on a moored barge which reduces the navigable width of any channel to less than 80 meters?
    - A. A white light placed on the two corners farthest from the bank
    - B. Two yellow lights in a vertical line at the stern
    - C. A red light placed on all four corners
    - D. A red light placed on the two corners farthest from the bank

23. BOTH INTERNATIONAL & INLAND. For identification purposes at night, U.S. Navy submarines on the surface may display an intermittent flashing light of which color?
    - A. Amber (yellow)   C. Blue
    - B. White   D. Red

24. BOTH INTERNATIONAL & INLAND. Which of the following would be "special circumstances" under the Rules?
    - A. Vessel at anchor
    - B. More than two vessels meeting
    - C. Speed in fog
    - D. Two vessels crossing

25. BOTH INTERNATIONAL & INLAND. The Navigation Rules define a "vessel not under command" as a vessel which _____.
    - A. from the nature of her work is unable to keep out of the way of another vessel
    - B. through some exceptional circumstance is unable to maneuver as required by the Rules
    - C. by taking action contrary to the Rules has created a "special circumstances" situation
    - D. is moored, aground, or anchored in a fairway

26. BOTH INTERNATIONAL & INLAND. Which statement is true concerning a "vessel engaged in fishing"?
    - A. The vessel may be using nets, lines, or trawls.
    - B. The vessel may be trolling.
    - C. The vessel is classified as "restricted in her ability to maneuver."
    - D. It sounds the same fog signal as a vessel underway but stopped.

27. BOTH INTERNATIONAL & INLAND. To be considered "engaged in fishing" according to the Rules of the Road, a vessel must be _____.
    A. using fishing apparatus which restricts maneuverability
    B. using trolling lines
    C. power-driven
    D. showing lights or shapes for a vessel restricted in her ability to manuever

28. BOTH INTERNATIONAL & INLAND. A vessel "restricted in her ability to maneuver" is one which _____.
    A. from the nature of her work is unable to maneuver as required by the Rules
    B. through some exceptional circumstance is unable to manuever as required by the Rules
    C. due to adverse weather conditions is unable to maneuver as required by the Rules
    D. has lost steering and is unable to maneuver

29. BOTH INTERNATIONAL & INLAND. You are on a vessel that cannot comply with the spacing requirement for masthead lights due to the nature of the vessel's function. What is required in this situation?
    A. The vessel must carry only the lights that comply with the Rules; the others may be omitted.
    B. The vessel's lights must comply as closely as possible, as determined by her government.
    C. The vessel must be altered to permit full compliance with the Rules.
    D. An all-round light should be substituted for the aft masthead light and the sternlight

30. BOTH INTERNATIONAL & INLAND. Which factor is listed in the Rules as one which must be taken into account when determining safe speed?
    A. The construction of the vessel
    B. The maneuverability of the vessel
    C. The experience of vessel personnel
    D. All of the above

31. BOTH INTERNATIONAL & INLAND. The Navigation Rules state that a vessel shall be operated at a safe speed at all times so that she can be stopped within _____.
    A. the distance of visibility
    B. 1/2 the distance of visibility
    C. a distance appropriate to the existing circumstances and conditions
    D. the distance that she would require for her propeller to go from full ahead to full astern

32. BOTH INTERNATIONAL & INLAND. Which statement is true concerning risk of collision?
    A. The stand-on vessel must keep out of the way of the other vessel when risk of collision exists.
    B. Risk of collision always exists when two vessels pass within one mile of each other.
    C. Risk of collision always exists when the compass bearing of an approaching vessel appreciably changes.
    D. Risk of collision may exist when the compass bearing of an approaching vessel is changing appreciably.

33. BOTH INTERNATIONAL & INLAND. In which situation would you consider risk of collision to exist?
    A. A vessel is two points on your port bow, range increasing, bearing changing slightly to the right.
    B. A vessel is broad on your starboard beam, range decreasing, bearing changing rapidly to the right.
    C. A vessel is two points abaft your port beam, range increasing, bearing is constant.
    D. A vessel is on your starboard quarter, range decreasing, bearing is constant

34. BOTH INTERNATIONAL & INLAND. In order for there to be risk of collision, which condition(s) must be true?
    A. The other vessel must be approaching
    B. Your vessel must be making way.
    C. The other vessel must be forward of your beam.
    D. All of the above

35. BOTH INTERNATIONAL & INLAND. You are approaching another vessel. She is about one mile distant and is on your starboard bow. You believe she will cross ahead of you. She then sounds a whistle signal of five short blasts. You should _____.
    A. answer the signal and hold course and speed
    B. reduce speed slightly to make sure she will have room to pass
    C. make a large course change, and slow down if necessary
    D. wait for another whistle signal from the other vessel

36. BOTH INTERNATIONAL & INLAND. Which of the following is a requirement for any action taken to avoid collision?
    A. When in sight of another vessel, any action taken must be accompanied by sound signals.
    B. The action taken must include changing the speed of the vessel.
    C. The action must be positive and made in ample time.
    D. All of the above

37. BOTH INTERNATIONAL & INLAND. A sailing vessel is meeting a vessel fishing in a narrow channel. Which statement is true?
    A. The fishing vessel is directed not to impede the passage of the sail vessel.
    B. The fishing vessel has the right-of-way.
    C. Each vessel should move to the edge of the channel on her port side.
    D. Each vessel should be displaying signals for a vessel constrained by her draft.

38. BOTH INTERNATIONAL & INLAND. Which vessel is not to impede the passage of a vessel which can only navigate safely within a narrow channel?
    A. Any vessel less than 20 meters in length
    B. Any sailing vessel
    C. A vessel engaged in fishing
    D. All of the above

39. BOTH INTERNATIONAL & INLAND. You are crossing a narrow channel in an 18-meter tug when you sight a tankship off your port bow coming up the channel. Which statement is correct?
    A. Neither vessel has the right-of-way because it is a crossing situation.
    B. You cannot impede the safe passage of the tankship.
    C. The tankship has the right-of-way because it is to port of your vessel.
    D. The tankship has the right-of-way because it is the larger of the two vessels.

40. BOTH INTERNATIONAL & INLAND. In narrow channels, vessels of less than what length shall not hamper the safe passage of vessels which can navigate only inside that channel?
    A. 20 meters   C. 65 meters
    B. 50 meters   D. 100 meters

41. BOTH INTERNATIONAL & INLAND. If two sailing vessels are running free with the wind on the same side, which one must keep clear of the other?
    A. The one with the wind closest abeam
    B. The one with the wind closest astern
    C. The one to leeward
    D. The one to windward

42. BOTH INTERNATIONAL & INLAND. A vessel is overtaking when she can see which lights of the vessel she is approaching?
    A. Only the sternlight of the vessel
    B. The sternlight and one sidelight of the vessel
    C. Only a sidelight of the vessel
    D. The masthead lights of the vessel

43. BOTH INTERNATIONAL & INLAND. The Rules state that, if there is any doubt as to whether a certain situation exists, it shall be considered to exist by the vessel in doubt. This principle applies to which situation?
    A. Risk of collision
    B. A vessel overtaking another vessel
    C. A vessel meeting another head on
    D. All of the above

44. BOTH INTERNATIONAL & INLAND. An overtaking situation occurs when one vessel approaches another from more than how many degrees abaft the beam?
    A. 0 degrees   C. 22.5 degrees
    B. 11.25 degrees   D. 45 degrees

45. BOTH INTERNATIONAL & INLAND. Which statement is true concerning an overtaking situation?
    A. It happens when one vessel is approaching another vessel from more than 20 degrees abaft the beam.
    B. It is the duty of the vessel being overtaken to get out of the way.
    C. Any later change of bearing between the two vessels shall not make the overtaking vessel a crossing vessel.
    D. All of the above

46. BOTH INTERNATIONAL & INLAND. Which statement correctly applies to a situation where a sailing vessel is overtaking a power-driven vessel?
   A. The power-driven vessel must keep out of the way of the sailing vessel.
   B. A "special circumstances" situation exists.
   C. The sailing vessel must keep out of the way of the power-driven vessel.
   D. The vessel which has the other vessel to the right must keep out of the way.

47. BOTH INTERNATIONAL & INLAND. Vessel A is on course 000 True. Vessel B is on a head-on course and is bearing 355 True, 200 yards away from Vessel A. To ensure a safe passing, Vessel A should _____.
   A. maintain course
   B. alter course to port
   C. alter course to ensure a starboard-to-starboard passing
   D. maneuver to ensure a port-to-port passing

48. BOTH INTERNATIONAL & INLAND. In which situation do the Rules require both vessels to change course?
   A. Two power-driven vessels meeting head-on
   B. Two power-driven vessels crossing when it is apparent to the stand-on vessel that the give-way vessel is not taking appropriate action
   C. Two sailing vessels crossing with the wind on the same side
   D. All of the above

49. BOTH INTERNATIONAL & INLAND. When two power-driven vessels are crossing, which vessel is the stand-on vessel?
   A. The vessel which is to starboard of the other vessel
   B. The vessel which is to port of the other vessel
   C. The larger vessel
   D. The vessel that sounds the first whistle signal

50. BOTH INTERNATIONAL & INLAND. While navigating a power-driven vessel at night, you sight the red sidelight of another vessel on your port bow. Its after masthead light is to the right of the forward masthead light. You should _____.
   A. hold course and speed
   B. alter course to port
   C. stop engines
   D. sound the danger signal

51. BOTH INTERNATIONAL & INLAND. When two power-driven vessels are crossing, the vessel which has the other to starboard must keep out of the way if _____.
   A. she is the faster vessel
   B. the situation involves risk of collision
   C. the vessels will pass within one-half mile of each other
   D. whistle signals have been sounded

52. BOTH INTERNATIONAL & INLAND. Every vessel that is to keep out of the way of another vessel must take positive early action to comply with this obligation and must _____.
   A. avoid crossing ahead of the other vessel
   B. avoid passing astern of the other vessel
   C. sound one prolonged blast to indicate compliance
   D. alter course to port for a vessel on her port side

53. BOTH INTERNATIONAL & INLAND. Your vessel is NOT making way, but is not in any way disabled. Another vessel is approaching you on your starboard beam. Which statement is true?
    A. The other vessel must give way since your vessel is stopped.
    B. Your vessel is the give-way vessel in a crossing situation.
    C. You should be showing the lights or shapes for a vessel not under command.
    D. You should be showing the lights or shapes for a vessel restricted in her ability to maneuver.

54. BOTH INTERNATIONAL & INLAND. Which of the following must be true in order for a stand-on vessel to take action to avoid collision by her maneuver alone?
    A. She must be in sight of the give-way vessel.
    B. There must be risk of collision.
    C. She must determine that the give-way vessel is not taking appropriate action.
    D. All of the above

55. BOTH INTERNATIONAL & INLAND. When is a stand-on vessel first allowed by the Rules to take action in order to avoid collision?
    A. When the two vessels are less than one-half mile from each other
    B. When the give-way vessel is not taking appropriate action to avoid collision
    C. When collision is imminent
    D. The stand-on vessel is not allowed to take action at any time.

56. BOTH INTERNATIONAL & INLAND. Which requirement must be met in order for a stand-on vessel to take action to avoid collision in accordance with Rule 17?
    A. Risk of collision must have been deemed to exist.
    B. The give-way vessel must have taken no action.
    C. The vessels must be within one-half mile of each other.
    D. There are no requirements to be met. The stand-on vessel may take action anytime.

57. BOTH INTERNATIONAL & INLAND. In a crossing situation in which you are the stand-on vessel, you must hold your course and speed until _____.
    A. the other vessel takes necessary action
    B. the other vessel gets to within one-half mile of your vessel
    C. action by the give-way vessel alone will not prevent collision
    D. the other vessel gets to within one-quarter mile of your vessel.

58. BOTH INTERNATIONAL & INLAND. You are in charge of a stand-on vessel in a crossing situation. The other vessel is 1.5 miles to port. You have determined that risk of collision exists. You should _____.
    A. take avoiding action immediately upon determining that risk of collision exists
    B. immediately sound the danger signal
    C. take avoiding action only after providing the give-way vessel time to take action, and determining that her action is not appropriate
    D. hold course and speed until the point of extremis, and then sound the danger signal, taking whatever action will best avert a collision

59. BOTH INTERNATIONAL & INLAND. You are the watch officer on a power-driven vessel and notice a large sail vessel approaching from astern. You should _____.
   A. slow down
   B. sound one short blast and change course to starboard
   C. sound two short blasts and change course to port
   D. hold course and speed

60. BOTH INTERNATIONAL & INLAND. Two power-driven vessels are crossing so as to involve risk of collision. Which statement is true, according to the Rules?
   A. The vessel which has the other on her port side shall keep out of the way.
   B. If the stand-on vessel takes action, she shall avoid changing course to port.
   C. If the give-way vessel takes action, she shall avoid changing course to starboard.
   D. The give-way vessel should keep the other vessel to her starboard.

61. BOTH INTERNATIONAL & INLAND. A vessel is underway and fishing with trolling lines. This vessel _____.
   A. must keep out of the way of sailing vessels when there is risk of collision
   B. must sound one prolonged, two short blast signal in restricted visibility
   C. is the stand-on vessel when overtaking power-driven vessels
   D. all of the above

62. BOTH INTERNATIONAL & INLAND. On open water, a fishing vessel is in a crossing situation with a sailing vessel located on the fishing vessel's starboard side. Which vessel is the stand-on vessel?
   A. The fishing vessel because it is to port of the sailing vessel
   B. The fishing vessel because it is fishing
   C. The sailing vessel because it is to starboard of the fishing vessel
   D. The sailing vessel because it is sailing

63. BOTH INTERNATIONAL & INLAND. Which statement is true, according to the Rules?
   A. A fishing vessel has the right-of-way over a vessel constrained by her draft.
   B. A vessel not under command shall avoid impeding the safe passage of a vessel constrained by her draft.
   C. A vessel engaged in fishing shall, so far as possible, keep out of the way of a vessel restricted in her ability to maneuver.
   D. A vessel restricted in her ability to maneuver shall keep out of the way of a vessel not under command.

64. BOTH INTERNATIONAL & INLAND. In restricted visibility, a vessel which detects by radar alone the presence of another vessel shall determine if a close-quarters situation is developing or risk of collision exists. If so, she shall _____.
   A. sound the danger signal
   B. when taking action make only course changes
   C. avoid altering course toward a vessel abaft the beam
   D. all of the above

65. BOTH INTERNATIONAL & INLAND. You are in charge of a power-driven vessel in dense fog. You observe another vessel on radar who is one-half mile distant on your port bow. You should _____.
 A. sound the danger signal
 B. exchange passing signals
 C. sound one long blast
 D. make no change in your fog signal

66. BOTH INTERNATIONAL & INLAND. Which vessel is the stand-on vessel when two vessels on a crossing course in fog are not in sight of one another?
 A. The vessel which has the other on her own starboard side
 B. The vessel which has the other on her own port side
 C. The one which hears the other's fog signal first
 D. Neither is the stand-on vessel

67. BOTH INTERNATIONAL & INLAND. In fog you observe your radar and determine that risk of collision exists with a vessel which is 2 miles off your port bow. You should _____.
 A. stop your engines
 B. sound the danger signal at two-minute intervals
 C. hold course and speed until the other vessel is sighted
 D. take proper avoiding action as soon as possible

68. BOTH INTERNATIONAL & INLAND. A lantern combining the two side-lights of a vessel's running lights may be shown on a _____.
 A. sailing vessel of 25 meters in length
 B. 20-meter vessel engaged in fishing, and making way
 C. 25-meter power-driven vessel engaged in trolling
 D. 6-meter vessel under oars

69. BOTH INTERNATIONAL & INLAND. A lantern combining the two side-lights of a vessel's running lights may be shown on a _____.
 A. 10-meter sailing vessel
 B. 20-meter vessel engaged in fishing, and making way
 C. 25-meter power-driven vessel engaged in trolling
 D. 25-meter pilot vessel

70. BOTH INTERNATIONAL & INLAND. You see a vessel's green sidelight bearing due east from you. The vessel might be heading _____.
 A. east   C. northwest
 B. northeast   D. southwest

71. BOTH INTERNATIONAL & INLAND. You see a red sidelight bearing NW. That vessel may be heading _____.
 A. south   C. northeast
 B. east   D. west

72. BOTH INTERNATIONAL & INLAND. A towing light, according to the Rules, is a _____.
 A. white light   C. yellow light
 B. red light   D. blue light

73. BOTH INTERNATIONAL & INLAND. The masthead light may be located at other than the fore-and-aft centerline of a vessel _____.
 A. less than 20 meters in length
 B. less than 12 meters in length
 C. which has separate sidelights carried on the outboard extremes of the vessel's breadth
 D. engaged in fishing

74. BOTH INTERNATIONAL & INLAND. A "flashing light," according to the
    definition given in the Rules, is a light that _____.
    A. is red in color
    B. is visible over an arc of the horizon of 360 degrees
    C. flashes at regular intervals at a frequency of 120 flashes or
       more per minute
    D. all of the above

75. INTERNATIONAL ONLY. Lighting requirements in inland waters are
    different from those for international waters for _____.
    A. barges being pushed ahead
    B. vessels constrained by their draft
    C. a vessel towing by pushing ahead
    D. all of the above

76. INTERNATIONAL ONLY. Which vessel may NOT exhibit two red lights in
    a vertical line?
    A. A vessel constrained by her draft
    B. A trawler
    C. A vessel aground
    D. A dredge

77. BOTH INTERNATIONAL & INLAND. A power-driven vessel less than 12
    meters in length may, instead of the underway lights for vessels under
    50 meters, at night, show which of the following?
    A. Sidelights and a sternlight
    B. One all-round white light and sidelights
    C. Masthead light only
    D. Sternlight only

78. BOTH INTERNATIONAL & INLAND. Which vessel must show forward and
    after masthead lights when making way?
    A. A 75-meter vessel restricted in her ability to maneuver
    B. A 100-meter sailing vessel
    C. A 150-meter vessel engaged in fishing
    D. A 45-meter vessel engaged in towing

79. BOTH INTERNATIONAL & INLAND. Two barges are being pushed ahead
    by a towboat. Which statement is true concerning lights on the barges?
    A. Each vessel should show sidelights.
    B. Each vessel should show at least one white light.
    C. The barges should be lighted as separate units.
    D. The barges should be lighted as one vessel.

80. BOTH INTERNATIONAL & INLAND. Which vessel would exhibit sidelights
    when underway and not making way?
    A. A vessel towing astern
    B. A vessel trawling
    C. A vessel not under command
    D. A vessel engaged in dredging operations

81. BOTH INTERNATIONAL & INLAND. A power-driven vessel when towing
    another vessel astern (tow less than 200 meters) shall show _____.
    A. two masthead lights in a vertical line instead of the forward
       masthead light
    B. two masthead lights in a vertical line instead of either the
       forward or after masthead lights
    C. two towing lights in a vertical line at the stern
    D. a small white light abaft the funnel

82. BOTH INTERNATIONAL & INLAND. A 20-meter vessel is towing another vessel astern. The length of the tow from the stern of the towing vessel to the stern of the tow is 75 meters. How many white towing identification lights shall the towing vessel show at night?

    A. 1   C. 3

    B. 2   D. 4

83. BOTH INTERNATIONAL & INLAND. A 50-meter vessel is towing astern and the length of the tow is 100 meters. In addition to sidelights, she may show _____.

    A. two masthead lights forward, a sternlight, and a towing light above the sternlight

    B. a masthead light forward, two masthead lights aft, a sternlight, and a towing light above the sternlight

    C. no masthead light forward, two masthead lights aft, a sternlight, and a towing light above the sternlight

    D. three masthead lights forward, one masthead light aft, and two towing lights in a vertical line at the stern

84. BOTH INTERNATIONAL & INLAND. A 45-meter vessel is pulling a 210-meter tow. She may exhibit _____.

    A. a masthead light forward and two masthead lights in a vertical line aft

    B. three masthead lights forward and one aft

    C. two masthead lights forward and no masthead light aft

    D. none of the above

85. BOTH INTERNATIONAL & INLAND. What lights, if any, would you exhibit at night if your vessel were broken down and being towed by another vessel?

    A. None

    B. Same lights as for a power-driven vessel underway

    C. A white light forward and a white light aft

    D. The colored sidelights and a white sternlight

86. BOTH INTERNATIONAL & INLAND. A partly submerged vessel or object being towed, which is not readily noticeable, shall show _____.

    A. yellow lights at each end

    B. two red lights in a vertical line

    C. a black ball

    D. a diamond shape

87. BOTH INTERNATIONAL & INLAND. A sailing vessel of over 20 meters in length underway must show a _____.

    A. red light over a green light at the masthead

    B. white masthead light

    C. combined lantern

    D. sternlight

88. BOTH INTERNATIONAL & INLAND. A 15-meter sailing vessel would be required to show _____.

    A. sidelights, a sternlight, and a red light over a green light on the mast

    B. sidelights and sternlight, but they may be in a combined lantern on the mast

    C. separate sidelights and a sternlight

    D. sidelights only

89. BOTH INTERNATIONAL & INLAND. Which vessel may carry her sidelights and sternlight in a combined lantern on the mast?
    A. An 18-meter sailing vessel
    B. A 10-meter sailing vessel also being propelled by machinery
    C. A 25-meter sailing vessel
    D. All of the above

90. BOTH INTERNATIONAL & INLAND. A lantern combining the two side-lights of a vessel's running lights may be shown on a _____.
    A. 15-meter sailing vessel
    B. 20-meter vessel engaged in fishing, and making way
    C. 25-meter power-driven vessel trolling
    D. 25-meter pilot vessel

91. BOTH INTERNATIONAL & INLAND. Which vessel shall turn off her sidelights?
    A. Any vessel that is not under command
    B. Any fishing vessel that is not making way
    C. Any sailing vessel when becalmed
    D. Any vessel engaged in underwater operations

92. BOTH INTERNATIONAL & INLAND. Which vessel must show a masthead light abaft of and higher than her identifying lights?
    A. A 55-meter vessel fishing
    B. A 55-meter vessel trawling
    C. A 100-meter vessel not under command
    D. A 20-meter vessel engaged in pilotage duty

93. BOTH INTERNATIONAL & INLAND. A vessel engaged in fishing during the day would show _____.
    A. one black ball
    B. two cones with bases together
    C. a cone, point downward
    D. two cones, points together

94. BOTH INTERNATIONAL & INLAND. You see a vessel displaying a basket in the rigging. It could be a _____.
    A. 100-meter vessel engaged in fishing
    B. 30-meter vessel trawling
    C. 15-meter vessel trolling
    D. 15-meter vessel engaged in fishing while at anchor

95. BOTH INTERNATIONAL & INLAND. A vessel engaged in a towing opera-tion which severely restricts the towing vessel and her tow in their ability to deviate from their course shall, when making way, show _____.
    A. the lights for a towing vessel
    B. the lights for a vessel restricted in its ability to maneuver
    C. sidelights and sternlight
    D. all of the above

96. BOTH INTERNATIONAL & INLAND. A vessel restricted in her ability to maneuver shall _____.
    A. turn off her sidelights when not making way
    B. when operating in restricted visibility sound a whistle signal of two prolonged and one short blast
    C. show a day shape of two diamonds in a vertical line
    D. keep out of the way of a vessel engaged in fishing

97. BOTH INTERNATIONAL & INLAND. A vessel restricted in her ability to
maneuver which is at anchor must show at night which of the
following lights?
   A. A red, a white, and a red light in a vertical line, and anchor
      lights
   B. A red, a white, and a red light in a vertical line only
   C. Anchor lights only
   D. Anchor lights and sidelights only

98. BOTH INTERNATIONAL & INLAND. A vessel which is unable to maneuver
due to some exceptional circumstance shall show two red lights in a
vertical line and, _____.
   A. during the day, three balls in a vertical line
   B. during the day, three shapes, the highest and lowest being balls
      and the middle being a diamond
   C. when making way at night, sidelights and a sternlight
   D. when making way at night, masthead lights, sidelights, and a
      sternlight

99. BOTH INTERNATIONAL & INLAND. Which vessel would have no white
lights visible when meeting her head on?
   A. A vessel trawling
   B. A vessel restricted in her ability to maneuver
   C. A vessel mineclearing
   D. A vessel not under command.

100. BOTH INTERNATIONAL & INLAND. By day, when it is impracticable
for a small vessel engaged in diving operations to display the shapes
for a vessel engaged in underwater operations, it shall display
_____.
   A. three black balls in a vertical line
   B. two red balls in a vertical line
   C. a black cylinder
   D. a rigid replica of the International Code flag "A"

101. BOTH INTERNATIONAL & INLAND. A pilot vessel on pilotage duty at
night will show sidelights and a sternlight _____.
   A. when at anchor
   B. only when making way
   C. at any time when underway
   D. only when the identifying lights are not being shown

102. BOTH INTERNATIONAL & INLAND. What is the minimum length of an
anchored vessel which is required to show a white light both
forward and aft?
   A. 50 meters   C. 150 meters
   B. 100 meters   D. 200 meters

103. BOTH INTERNATIONAL & INLAND. Which vessel must have a gong, or
other equipment which will make the sound of a gong?
   A. A sailing vessel
   B. Any vessel over 50 meters
   C. Any vessel over 100 meters
   D. A power-driven vessel over 75 meters

104. BOTH INTERNATIONAL & INLAND. What is the minimum sound-signaling equipment required aboard a vessel 10 meters in length?
    A. A bell only
    B. A whistle only
    C. A bell and a whistle
    D. Any means of making an efficient sound signal

105. BOTH INTERNATIONAL & INLAND. A vessel 25 meters in length is required to have onboard which of the following sound signaling appliances?
    A. None is required   C. Whistle and bell only
    B. Whistle only   D. Whistle, bell, and gong

106. BOTH INTERNATIONAL & INLAND. Which of the following statements is true concerning the danger signal?
    A. Vessels must be in sight of each other in order to use the danger signal.
    B. Only the stand-on vessel can sound the danger signal.
    C. Distress signals may be used in place of the danger signal.
    D. The danger signal consists of 4 or more short blasts of the whistle.

107. BOTH INTERNATIONAL & INLAND. A pilot vessel may continue to sound an identity signal in fog if she is _____.
    A. aground
    B. at anchor
    C. not under command
    D. no longer on pilotage duty

108. BOTH INTERNATIONAL & INLAND. At anchor in fog, the fog signal of another vessel underway has been steadily growing louder and the danger of collision appears to exist. In addition to the required fog signal, what signal may be used to indicate the presence of your vessel?
    A. The danger signal—five or more rapid blasts on the whistle
    B. Three blasts on the whistle: one short, one prolonged, and one short
    C. Three blasts on the whistle: one prolonged followed by two short
    D. No other signal may be used.

109. BOTH INTERNATIONAL & INLAND. When should the fog signal of a vessel being towed be sounded?
    A. After the towing vessel's fog signal
    B. Before the towing vessel's fog signal
    C. Approximately one minute after the towing vessel's fog signal
    D. If the towing vessel is sounding a fog signal, the vessel towed is not required to sound any fog signal.

110. BOTH INTERNATIONAL & INLAND. While underway in fog you hear the rapid ringing of a bell for about five seconds followed by the sounding of a gong for about five seconds. This signal came from a _____.
    A. vessel fishing
    B. seaplane anchored
    C. vessel over 100 meters in length at anchor
    D. vessel aground

111. BOTH INTERNATIONAL & INLAND. While underway in fog, you hear a
vessel ahead sound two blasts on the whistle. You should _____.
    A. sound two blasts and change course to the left
    B. sound whistle signals only if you change course
    C. sound only fog signals until the other vessel is sighted
    D. not sound any whistle signals until the other vessel is
       sighted

112. BOTH INTERNATIONAL & INLAND. A vessel 50 meters in length, at
anchor, is required to sound which of the following fog signals?
    A. 5-second ringing of a bell every minute
    B. 5-second ringing of a bell every two minutes
    C. 5-second sounding of a gong every minute
    D. 5-second sounding of both a bell and a gong every two
       minutes

113. BOTH INTERNATIONAL & INLAND. When underway in fog, you might
hear any of the following fog signals EXCEPT _____.
    A. one prolonged blast at intervals of one minute
    B. two prolonged blasts at intervals of one minute
    C. one prolonged and two short blasts at intervals of two
       minutes
    D. ringing of a bell for five seconds at intervals of two minutes

114. BOTH INTERNATIONAL & INLAND. Which vessel sounds the same fog
signal when underway or at anchor?
    A. A sailing vessel
    B. A vessel restricted in her ability to maneuver
    C. A vessel constrained by her draft
    D. A vessel not under command

115. BOTH INTERNATIONAL & INLAND. A vessel engaged in fishing while at
anchor shall sound a fog signal of _____.
    A. one prolonged and two short blasts at two-minute intervals
    B. one prolonged and three short blasts at two-minute intervals
    C. a rapid ringing of the bell for five seconds at one-minute
       intervals
    D. a sounding of the bell and gong at one-minute intervals

116. BOTH INTERNATIONAL & INLAND. You are underway in fog and you
hear three distinct bell strokes followed by five seconds of rapid bell
ringing followed by three distinct bell strokes. This signal indicates a
vessel _____.
    A. aground
    B. engaged in underwater construction
    C. at anchor
    D. in distress

117. BOTH INTERNATIONAL & INLAND. Your vessel enters fog. You stop
your engines, and the vessel is dead in the water. What fog signal
should you sound?
    A. One prolonged blast every two minutes
    B. Two prolonged blasts every two minutes
    C. Three short blasts every two minutes
    D. One prolonged and two short blasts every two minutes

118. BOTH INTERNATIONAL & INLAND. Which vessel must sound its fog signal at intervals not to exceed one minute?
    A. A power-driven vessel underway, not making way
    B. A vessel constrained by her draft
    C. A sailing vessel
    D. A vessel aground

119. BOTH INTERNATIONAL & INLAND. If underway in low visibility sounding fog signals, what changes would you make in the fog signal immediately upon losing the power plant?
    A. Begin sounding two prolonged blasts at two-minute intervals.
    B. Begin sounding one prolonged blast followed by three short blasts at two-minute intervals.
    C. Begin sounding one prolonged blast followed by two short blasts at two-minute intervals.
    D. No change should be made in the fog signal.

120. BOTH INTERNATIONAL & INLAND. A vessel engaged in fishing, underway, sounds the same fog signal as a _____.
    A. power-driven vessel stopped and making no way through the water
    B. vessel being towed
    C. vessel restricted in her ability to maneuver, at anchor
    D. sailing vessel at anchor

121. BOTH INTERNATIONAL & INLAND. Which vessel is required to sound a fog signal of one prolonged followed by two short blasts?
    A. A vessel not under command
    B. A sailing vessel, underway
    C. A vessel restricted in its ability to maneuver, at anchor
    D. All of the above

122. BOTH INTERNATIONAL & INLAND. In restricted visibility, a vessel restricted in her ability to maneuver, at anchor, would sound a fog signal of _____.
    A. the rapid ringing of a bell for five seconds every minute
    B. two prolonged and two short blasts every two minutes
    C. one prolonged and two short blasts every two minutes
    D. two prolonged and one short blast every two minutes

123. BOTH INTERNATIONAL & INLAND. The wind is ESE, and a sailing vessel is steering NW. What tack is she on, and what fog signal should she sound?
    A. Port tack; one blast at one-minute intervals
    B. Starboard tack; one blast at one-minute intervals
    C. Starboard tack; two blasts at one-minute intervals
    D. Starboard tack; one prolonged and two short blasts at two-minute intervals

124. BOTH INTERNATIONAL & INLAND. A sailing vessel with the wind aft of the beam is navigating in restricted visibility. She should sound _____.
    A. three short blasts
    B. one prolonged blast
    C. one prolonged and two short blasts
    D. two prolonged blasts

125. BOTH INTERNATIONAL & INLAND. Which signal, other than a distress signal, can be used by a vessel to attract attention?
      A. searchlight
      B. continuous sounding of a fog signaling apparatus
      C. burning barrel
      D. orange smoke signal
126. BOTH INTERNATIONAL & INLAND. A vessel may use any sound or light signals to attract the attention of another vessel as long as _____.
      A. white lights are not used
      B. red and green lights are not used
      C. the vessel signals such intentions over the radiotelephone
      D. the signal cannot be mistaken for a signal authorized by the Rules
127. BOTH INTERNATIONAL & INLAND. All of the following are distress signals under the Rules EXCEPT _____.
      A. a green star signal
      B. orange-colored smoke
      C. red flares
      D. the repeated raising and lowering of outstretched arms
128. BOTH INTERNATIONAL & INLAND. All of the following are distress signals EXCEPT _____.
      A. the continuous sounding of any fog signaling apparatus
      B. giving five or more short and rapid blasts of the whistle
      C. firing a gun at intervals of about a minute
      D. a barrel with burning oil in it on deck
129. BOTH INTERNATIONAL & INLAND. Vessels engaged in fishing may show the additional signals described in Annex II to the Rules when they _____.
      A. desire to do so
      B. are fishing in a traffic separation zone
      C. are in a narrow channel
      D. are in close proximity to other vessels engaged in fishing
130. BOTH INTERNATIONAL & INLAND. Which of the following signals may at some time be exhibited by a vessel trawling?
      A. Two white lights in a vertical line
      B. A white light over a red light in a vertical line
      C. Two red lights in a vertical line
      D. Any of the above
131. INTERNATIONAL ONLY. Which statement is true concerning a vessel "constrained by her draft"?
      A. She must be a power-driven vessel.
      B. She is not under command.
      C. She may be a vessel being towed.
      D. She is hampered because of her work.
132. INTERNATIONAL ONLY. Which of the following vessels is NOT regarded as being "restricted in her ability to maneuver"?
      A. a vessel servicing an aid to navigation
      B. a vessel engaged in dredging
      C. a towing vessel with tow unable to deviate from its course
      D. a vessel constrained by her draft

133. INTERNATIONAL ONLY. You are operating a vessel through a narrow channel and your vessel must stay within the channel to be navigated safely. Another vessel is crossing your course from starboard to port, and you are in doubt as to his intentions. You _____.

A. may sound the danger signal
B. must sound the danger signal
C. should sound one short blast to indicate that you are holding course and speed
D. are required to back down

134. INTERNATIONAL ONLY. You are in charge of a 250-meter freight vessel proceeding down a narrow channel. There is a vessel engaged in fishing on your starboard bow one-half mile away. Which statement is true?

A. You are not to impede the fishing vessel.
B. If you are in doubt as to the fishing vessel's movement, you may sound the danger signal.
C. You are to slow to bare steerageway until clear of the fishing vessel.
D. You must sound the danger signal.

135. INTERNATIONAL ONLY. There are two classes of vessels which do not have to comply with the rule regarding traffic separation schemes, to the extent necessary to carry out their work. One of these is a vessel _____.

A. engaged in fishing
B. servicing a submarine cable
C. towing another
D. in pilotage duty

136. INTERNATIONAL ONLY. You are approaching another vessel and will pass starboard to starboard without danger if no course changes are made. You should _____.

A. hold course and sound a two-blast whistle signal
B. hold course and sound no whistle signal
C. change course to the right and sound one blast
D. hold course and sound one blast

137. INTERNATIONAL ONLY. Which of the following statements is correct concerning a situation involving a fishing vessel and a vessel not under command?

A. The fishing vessel must keep clear of the vessel not under command.
B. If the vessel not under command is a power-driven vessel, it must keep clear of the fishing vessel.
C. They must exchange whistle signals.
D. Both vessels are required to take action to stay clear of each other.

138. INTERNATIONAL ONLY. Which vessel shall avoid impeding the safe passage of a vessel constrained by her draft?

A. A vessel not under command
B. A fishing vessel
C. A vessel restricted in her ability to maneuver
D. All of the above

139. INTERNATIONAL ONLY. When two vessels are meeting, a two-blast whistle signal by either of the vessels indicates _____.
   A. "I intend to alter course to port."
   B. "I desire to pass starboard to starboard."
   C. "I desire to pass port to port."
   D. "I am altering course to port."

140. INTERNATIONAL ONLY. Which signal may be sounded by one of two vessels in sight of each other?
   A. Four short blasts on the whistle
   B. One prolonged blast on the whistle
   C. One short blast on the whistle followed by one flash of a light
   D. One short, one prolonged, and one short blast on the whistle

141. INTERNATIONAL ONLY. Which signal is only sounded by a power-driven vessel?
   A. A signal meaning "I am altering my course to starboard"
   B. A signal meaning "I intend to overtake you on your starboard side"
   C. A signal meaning that the vessel sounding it is in doubt as to the other vessel's actions
   D. A signal sounded when approaching a bend

142. INTERNATIONAL ONLY. When moving from a berth alongside a quay (wharf), a vessel must sound _____.
   A. a prolonged blast   C. a long blast
   B. three short blasts   D. none of the above

143. INTERNATIONAL ONLY. Vessel A is overtaking Vessel B on open waters and will pass without changing course. Vessel A _____.
   A. should sound two short blasts
   B. should sound the danger signal
   C. should sound one long blast
   D. need not sound any whistle signals

144. INTERNATIONAL ONLY. You are in sight of another vessel in a crossing situation, and the other vessel sounds one short blast. You are going to hold course and speed. You should _____.
   A. answer with one short blast
   B. answer with two short blasts
   C. sound the danger signal
   D. sound no whistle signal

145. INTERNATIONAL ONLY. A signal of one prolonged, one short, one prolonged, and one short blast, in that order, is given by a _____.
   A. pilot vessel   C. vessel at anchor
   B. vessel in distress   D. vessel being overtaken

146. INTERNATIONAL ONLY. You are underway in a narrow channel, and you are being overtaken by a vessel astern. After the overtaking vessel sounds the proper signal indicating his intention to pass your vessel on your starboard side, you signal your agreement by sounding _____.
   A. one short blast
   B. two prolonged blasts
   C. two prolonged followed by two short blasts
   D. one prolonged, one short, one prolonged, and one short blast, in that order

147. INTERNATIONAL ONLY. On open water two vessels are in an overtaking situation. The overtaking vessel has just sounded one short blast on the whistle. What is the meaning of this whistle signal?
    A. "I request permission to pass you on my port side."
    B. "I will maintain course and speed and pass you on your starboard side."
    C. "On which side should I pass?"
    D. "I am changing course to starboard."

148. INTERNATIONAL ONLY. A sailing vessel is overtaking a power-driven vessel in a narrow channel, so as to pass on the vessel's port side. The overtaken vessel will have to move to facilitate passage. The sailing vessel is the _____.
    A. stand-on vessel and would sound two short blasts
    B. give-way vessel and would sound no whistle signal
    C. stand-on vessel and would sound no whistle signal
    D. give-way vessel and would sound two prolonged blasts followed by two short blasts

149. INTERNATIONAL ONLY. You intend to overtake a vessel in a narrow channel, and you intend to pass along the vessel's port side. How should you signal your intention?
    A. No signal is necessary
    B. Two prolonged blasts
    C. Two short blasts
    D. Two prolonged followed by two short blasts

150. INTERNATIONAL ONLY. A vessel not under command sounds the same fog signal as a vessel _____.
    A. engaged in towing
    B. constrained by her draft
    C. under sail
    D. all of the above

ANSWER KEY FOR RULES OF THE ROAD QUESTIONS

1. D	31. C	61. A	91. B	121. D
2. D	32. D	62. B	92. B	122. C
3. C	33. D	63. C	93. D	123. D
4. B	34. A	64. C	94. D	124. C
5. C	35. C	65. D	95. D	125. A
6. B	36. C	66. D	96. A	126. D
7. D	37. A	67. D	97. A	127. A
8. A	38. D	68. D	98. C	128. B
9. B	39. B	69. A	99. D	129. D
10. D	40. A	70. D	100. D	130. D
11. C	41. D	71. A	101. C	131. A
12. C	42. A	72. C	102. A	132. D
13. C	43. D	73. B	103. C	133. A
14. A	44. C	74. C	104. D	134. B
15. B	45. C	75. D	105. C	135. B
16. C	46. C	76. A	106. A	136. B
17. B	47. D	77. B	107. B	137. A
18. D	48. A	78. A	108. B	138. B
19. B	49. A	79. D	109. A	139. D
20. B	50. A	80. A	110. C	140. C
21. A	51. B	81. B	111. C	141. A
22. A	52. A	82. B	112. A	142. D
23. A	53. B	83. B	113. D	143. D
24. B	54. D	84. B	114. B	144. D
25. B	55. B	85. D	115. A	145. D
26. A	56. A	86. D	116. A	146. D
27. A	57. C	87. D	117. B	147. D
28. A	58. C	88. B	118. D	148. D
29. B	59. D	89. A	119. C	149. D
30. B	60. B	90. A	120. C	150. D

APPENDIX B:

STUDY APPROACH OUTLINE FOR RULES OF THE ROAD

I. Definitions

   A. General—Rule 3
   B. Lights and shapes for these vessels—Rules 21 through 30
   C. Risk of collision—Rule 7
   D. Narrow channels—Rule 9
   E. Maneuvering situations—Rules 13, 14, 15
   F. Not to impede—Rule 8(f)
   G. Lights and shapes for vessels maneuvering, etc.—
      lighting table, pages 72-77
   H. Annexes

II. Application of Definitions to Rule 18

   A. Courtesy rule
   B. Pecking order

III. Placing Moving Vessels in the Picture

   A. Type of vessel you are on—Rule 3
   B. Type of vessel you are viewing
   C. Possibilities for resolving the situation—Rules 6, 7, 8
   D. Decision-making process

IV. Maneuvering Situations

   A. Overtaking—Rule 13
   B. Meeting—Rule 14
   C. Crossing—Rule 15

V. Duties of Stand-on and Give-way Vessels

   A. Risk of collision prerequisite
   B. Rule 12
   C. Rule 15
   D. Rule 16
   E. Rule 17

F. Sound signals for maneuvering—Rules 32, 33, 34
    1. Sound signals, Inland
    2. Sound signals, International
    3. Danger signal—Rule 34(d)

VI. Restricted Visibility

A. Sound signals—Rule 35
B. Maneuvering—Rule 19

VII. Not to Impede—Rule 8(f)

A. Vessels involved with this Rule—Rules 9, 10, 18
B. Contrast to right-of-way—Rules 9, 12, 13, 14(d), 15, 17(d), 18

VIII. Narrow Channels—Rule 9

A. Maneuvers
B. Sound signals
C. Not to impede
D. Western Rivers differences—Rules 9 and 14

IX. Applying Lights to Vessel Definitions in Maneuvering Situations

A. Running lights—Rule 23
B. Identification lights ⎫
C. Working lights   ⎬ Rules 24-30
                       ⎭

X. Rule 2(a) and (b)

INDEX

ABOUT THE AUTHORS

B. A. Farnsworth graduated from the United States Merchant Marine Academy in 1971 with a bachelor of science degree in marine transportation, and served as a Coast Guard marine inspector for four years. Since 1975, he has been with the United States Coast Guard licensing program, first as a subject matter specialist and now as a marine vessel operation specialist. He is presently with the Merchant Vessel Personnel Division of Coast Guard Headquarters.

Larry C. Young is a graduate of the United States Coast Guard Academy and holds a master's degree in business administration from Oklahoma City University. He served as officer of the deck and navigator aboard the USCGC *Jarvis* before joining the United States Coast Guard Institute in 1976. He served as a licensing examination specialist, concentrating on second and third mate examinations and the initial offshore supply vessel exams.

After leaving the institute, he moved into the testing and training field. He was involved in revamping the training program for the Coast Guard Auxiliary. He left the Coast Guard and took the position of manager, military testing, for the American Council on Education, becoming involved in GED testing internationally. He now operates Knowledge Assessment Service, a consulting company specializing in test preparation courses. He has developed courses to prepare for the Scholastic Aptitude Test (SAT), the Graduate Record Examinations (GRE), and the Graduate Management Admission Test (GMAT) that have been used in three state education programs.